Backgammon
the modern game

Backgammon
the modern game

TERENCE REESE
& ROBERT BRINIG

CORNERSTONE LIBRARY, NEW YORK

Reprinted 1979

Published by Cornerstone Library
A Simon & Schuster Subsidiary of
Gulf & Western Corporation

Simon & Schuster Building
1230 Avenue of the Americas
New York, New York 10020

This new Cornerstone Library edition is published by arrangement with Sterling Publishing Co., Inc. and is a complete and unabridged reprint of the original hardcover edition

ISBN 346-12311-9

Manufactured in the United States of America

Contents

Starting the game—Throwing a double—When there is a problem in making the full legal move—Entering from the bar with two or more men—The rule for bearing off—Ways of winning—The doubling cube—Stakes and scoring—Points of procedure

Pointers — Builders — Six-shooters — Tempters — Table of opening moves

What are the chances of hitting a man which is from 1 to 12 spaces away?—List of travelling shots—Effect of intervening points—Minimizing the chances of being hit—What are the chances of throwing one or more specific numbers?—Chances of entering one man from the bar—Chances of entering two men from the bar—

Making a critical point—Hitting a blot—Bringing in a builder—Taking care of the back men

Bearing off when there is no contact—Bearing off when there is contact—Bringing in

The detailed count of pips—The running check—The count by throws—The mirror method

A thought for backgammon:
The race is not always to the swift.

Foreword

The literature on backgammon, compared to that on bridge and chess, is minute to the point of non-existence. Most of the books we have seen—and we make no criticism of this—are little more than introductory works written at a rather slow pace for beginners.

Because of the dearth of intermediate and advanced books, there must be thousands of players who find it hard to improve beyond a certain stage. We believe our book will solve that problem. The first chapter is elementary; from then on, we make fair demands on the reader's co-operation. Some of the later chapters may seem difficult for players who have little or no experience, we realize that; but if they return to the text after a period of play, it will mean much more to them.

In a book of this sort there are innumerable opportunities for semantic error and for errors in calculation. For example, we may say 'the blot on W 7 is exposed to 22 shots', and the reader, very sensibly working it out for himself, may make the answer something different. It is worth remarking, therefore, that all the signs and figures and diagrams in this book have been confirmed by a three-way independent check. Barring an invasion of gremlins into the printing presses, they *are* correct. So, if you disagree, please check your calculation once again: is it possible that you may have overlooked some duplication of moves?

We spoke of a three-way check. The third member, apart from the authors, was Miss Michele Cohen, aged 7. At that age they don't make mistakes.

Terence Reese
Robert Brinig

Backgammon
the modern game

CHAPTER ONE

Your First Half Hour

Backgammon is one of the easiest games to learn. You can master the moves and play a game without infringing the rules after half an hour. Time yourself. Moreover, given a little application, some practice, and three or four readings of this book, you will be a better than average player in a fortnight. This is a very different timetable from, say, bridge, where it takes three months to play even a tolerable game and a newcomer remains a novice for at least a year.

But this is not the moment for a digression—we have promised that you will be able to play in thirty minutes from now. First, set up the board in the following way:

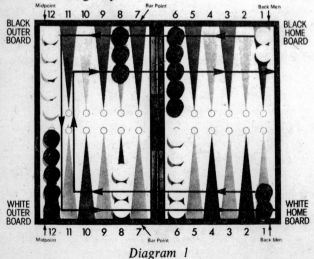

Diagram 1

You are looking at the board from White's angle. We have numbered the triangles—or 'points', as they are called—from 1 to 12 on each side of the table. As you can see from the arrows, White's two 'back men' start far away on B 1 (the triangle marked 1 on Black's side of the board). The W 7 and B 7 points, adjacent to the BAR (the centre strip), are called 'bar points', and the two 12 points, midway in the journey round the board, are called 'midpoints'. These terms are just a literary convenience, like North and South in a bridge diagram.

The four quarters—White Home Board, White Outer Board, Black Home Board, Black Outer Board—are also not marked on the board, but these divisions have a role in the game.

The opponents sit on opposite sides of the bar, one playing the White pieces, one the Black pieces (which in practice are often red). Each player has two dice, plus a cup from which he throws them. Finally, there is the big cube, known as the doubling cube. At a pinch, you can do without the cube or the cups, which are not always included in a travelling set.

As we have set up the pieces, White plays towards the home board on his right, Black towards his left. It is advisable to become equally accustomed to playing in either direction. On some boards the dark and light triangles may be the other way round; there is no fixed system.

Basically, backgammon is a race in which each player aims to move all his men round, and eventually off, the board. The player who achieves this first wins that particular game. The players in turn throw two dice and move one or more pieces the precise number of spaces indicated by the dice. Suppose you throw (or 'roll') 5–3. You may, subject to one important qualification (described below), move one man 5 spaces forward and another 3, or the same man 5 spaces, then 3, or 3, then 5. If you throw a double (two dice of the same number) you play *twice* the value of the throw (see page 17).

If there were no more to it than this, backgammon would be a simple game of chance. Three additional factors give the game its character:

13

1 There is a 'blocking' element. When a player has two or more men on a triangle he is said to have a POINT there. In no circumstances whatsoever may the opponent alight on that point, even in passing.

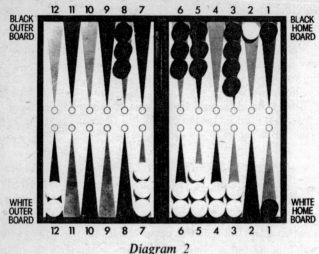

Diagram 2

Both players have a man in the opponent's home board, begging to be rescued. White throws 4–3. He would like to escape to B 9 but cannot do this because he would need to touch down on B 5 or B 6, and this he is not allowed to do. For the moment, he must move elsewhere on the board.

Black has a similar and rather more serious problem. There is only one way in which he can make progress at the back. He badly wants to throw 6–1; that would allow him to move from W 1 to W 2 and thence to W 8. If Black makes any other throw containing a 1 he can at least move from W 1 to W 2, so that a direct 6 will enable him to escape later.

2 There is a 'snakes and ladders' element. In the opening set-up (Diagram 1) there are two or more pieces on all the triangles that are occupied, but after a move or two there will be single pieces on some triangles. A single piece is called a BLOT, and when the opponent, moving his dice in accordance with the number thrown, alights on a blot, either settling there or passing on, this man is said to be HIT. He goes right back to the beginning and is placed on the bar. Furthermore, a player who has a man on the bar must bring it into his opponent's home board before he makes any other play. By throwing the appropriate number with one of his two dice he can bring the man into any vacant space or into a space which is occupied by *one* of his opponent's men (a hit) or any number of his own men. He cannot enter a space where his opponent holds a point. Thus, the more points you build in your home board, the more difficult you make it for your opponent to enter from the bar.

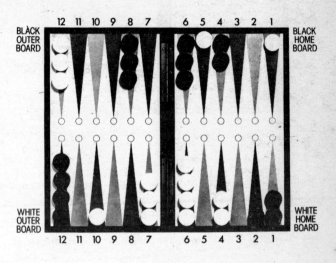

Diagram 3

White has three blots (lone men which are liable to be hit). Suppose that Black throws 5–4. He can hit in two ways—by moving one man from W 1 to W 10, or by moving one man from B 6 to B 1, making some other move with his 4. Alternatively, suppose that Black were to throw 4–3. He could then, with a man from his 8 point, hit the blot on B 5 and continue with the same man to hit on B 1, thus putting two men on the bar.

It is not too early to say that it is never obligatory to hit a blot (unless there is no other legal move) and that it would often be poor play to do so.

3 A player cannot bear off any of his men until he has shepherded his entire flock into his home board.

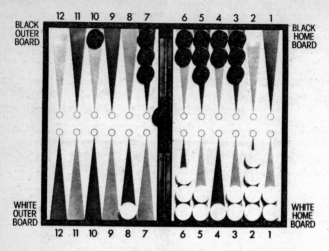

Diagram 4

White throws 5–4. Legally, he could make both moves within his home board, moving from 6 to 1 and from 5 to 1. That would leave blots on his 5 and 4 and would be exceptionally foolish, with Black taking aim from the bar. White is *not* allowed to bear off a man from his 5 and a man from his 4, because he has not yet brought all his men into his home board. There are various legal possibilities but only one sensible way to play the move: use the 4 to go from 8 to 4, covering the blot there, and use the 5, not to bear off a man, but to go from 6 to 1. Then no blot is left.

So now you understand the three factors that make the game a tactical struggle and not just a race. There are a few more points that must be mentioned before you can be said to know all the terms and procedure.

Starting the game

Each player throws one die only. (One tends to forget that dice is a plural word.) If the throw is a DOUBLE, such as two 4s, the doubling cube is turned to 2 and the stake for the game is automatically doubled.

If any more doubles are thrown they are ignored (though some gamblers like to go on turning the cube each time). As soon as each die is different, the player who has thrown the higher number makes the first play, using the number on his own die and the number on his opponent's die.

Throwing a double

A double is a special throw: you move not twice the number thrown, but four times. This is sometimes a delight, sometimes a disaster.

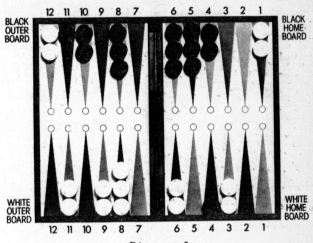

Diagram 5

White throws 3–3 (double 3). He must make four moves, each a 3, using one, two, three or four men to do it. Here he has numerous possibilities. He could move two men from W 8 to W 2; one from W 8 to W 2, one from W 9 to W 6, and one from B 12 to W 10; or one from B 12 to W 1, hitting a blot on the way. What he cannot do is move either man from B 1 to B 7, as this would involve touching down on B 4, where Black has a point.

When there is a problem in making the full legal move

Towards the end of a game a player's moves will often be restricted, in the sense that one or more of the numbers he has thrown will be unplayable. The rules are:

17

(a) He must make the full move if he can, but can choose the order. (This becomes relevant when bearing off.)

(b) If he can play only one number he makes just that move.

(c) Occasionally it will be possible to play either number but not both. In that case the higher number must be played.

(d) If he cannot make any legal move he misses his turn altogether.

All four situations are illustrated in Diagram 6:

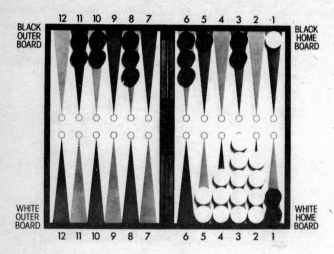

Diagram 6

Black, who has been hit several times, is way behind, but White still needs to bring out the man on B 1. White throws:

(a) 6–3. If he moves from B 1 to B 4 he will be unable to play the 6. He must, therefore, play from B 1 to B 7 and (unhappily) from W 5 to W 2.

(b) 5–2. He cannot move a 5 anywhere, nor 2–5. He just moves a 2, therefore.

(c) 6–4. White's first instinct is to hit the blot on B 5, but if he does that he cannot play the 6 afterwards. Since there is no way to play both numbers he must play the higher one, moving from B 1 to B 7.

(d) 5–5. He has no 5 anywhere on the board and so misses his turn.

18

Entering from the bar with two or more men

You will recall that when a player has a man on the bar he must bring it into play before he makes any other move. When he has two or more men on the bar he must bring them all in before he does anything else.

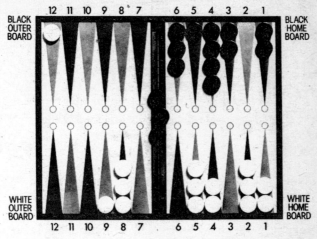

Diagram 7

Here Black has three men on the bar and White has four points in his home board. If Black throws any combination of 1 2 4 and 5 he is unable to play and misses his turn altogether. If he throws 5–3 he can bring one man into the 3 point but not make any other play. If he throws 6–3 he can bring in two men; the third stays on the bar. If he is lucky enough to throw 6–6 or 3–3 he can bring in all his men on the appropriate point and still has one further move to make.

The rule for bearing off

A player can bear men off, remember, only when they are all in his home board. He can bear off a man corresponding to the exact number of the throw—for example, if he throws 4–2 he can bear off a man from 4 and a man from 2. He may alternatively make any legitimate move within his home board. The special rule to remember is that if he throws a higher number than any point that he occupies in his home board he can—and must—move a man from the highest point that he does occupy. He may bear off this man or move it to a lower point and then bear off the highest man left.

19

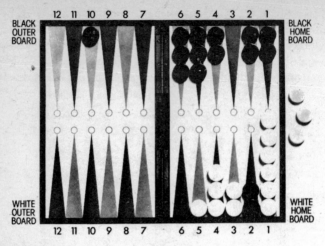

Diagram 8

White has already borne off three men and will be an easy winner so long as he can escape the attentions of the Black men on W 2. White throws:

(a) 4–1. He could bear off from 4 and from 1, but as that would leave the blot on W 5 it would be more sensible to bear off just the man on 5. Safer still, as a matter of fact, would be to move from 5 to 1 and from 4 to 3. If three men are left on the highest point, various throws become dangerous.

(b) 6–2. Having no man on 6, White must move from the highest point he does occupy. However, he is not obliged to bear off from 5 and then to move from 3 to 1, leaving a blot. He can make the 2 move first, from 5 to 3, and then bear off from 4.

(c) 3–3. This is a murderous throw. There are two ways of playing it: three men from 4 to 1 and bear off one from 3, leaving blots on 5 and 3; or two men from 4 to 1 and bear off two from 3, leaving blots on 5 and 4.

Ways of winning

The player who first bears off all his men wins a single game; but if a player bears off all his men before the opponent has borne off any, he wins a GAMMON, a double game. This has an important bearing on tactics.

20

Traditionally, there is a third form of winning: if at the end of the game the loser has not borne off any men and still has a man stranded in the winner's home board, or on the bar, he loses a BACKGAMMON, a triple game. This rule is going out of fashion, at any rate in Europe. The possibility of a backgammon has a confusing effect on tactics in the end game and, of course, backgammons bump up the stakes. We propose, in this book, to leave backgammons out of the reckoning. However, in a later chapter we include a paragraph explaining the effect when they are played.

The doubling cube

The doubling cube is a comparatively recent invention in the long life of backgammon. It has no effect on the mechanics of play, but it gives tremendous zip to the scoring.

At the beginning of the game the cube is set at an improbable 64 and is placed midway along the side of the board. As we have explained, it is turned to 2 when the first throw of the game (one die from each player) is a double. This is an 'automatic' as opposed to a 'voluntary' double.

At any point in the game a player whose turn it is to throw may turn the cube before he throws—to 2 if there was no double at the outset, to 4 if there was. He moves the cube to the opponent's side of the bar and the message is: 'You can resign and settle for the stake as it stands at the moment. But if you accept, the stakes are doubled'. If the opponent accepts he takes charge of the cube and only he can offer a subsequent double, should he judge that the game has turned in his favour. If this next double is accepted the cube reverts to the first player, who alone can offer the next double, and so it goes on. Not many games go beyond 8 points unless there is a gammon as well, but some do.

There is one further variation, which is optional but adds a little spice. If a player thinks that his opponent has offered a premature or ill-judged double he may turn the cube at once to the next number. This is called a BEAVER. Of course, a player who holds the cube may always redouble; the point of doing so at once, by beavering, is that he retains possession of the cube, a decided advantage.

The cube is not just a gambling device. It makes judgement of position a most important element in the game.

Stakes and scoring

Backgammon is a good enough game to be played for fun, but when there is no stake at all some elements of the game, such as accepting a double or avoiding a gammon, lose much of their point. No doubt some rivals may contest such a game with the utmost rigour for the simple pride of winning—but...er...we haven't met them.

It is usual to fix a unit representing the stake for a single game. In a series of games lasting a couple of hours anything over 20 points would be a big swing. Alternatively, you can play for a flat amount by following 'tournament rules'. You arrange to play, say, 'seven up', using the doubling cube and scoring doubled and redoubled games in the usual way. The player who first scores seven points is the winner. There are usually two special rules: automatic doubles are not played, and when one player has scored six points (one short of the total required) his opponent is not allowed to double in the game immediately following. Obviously the player in the lead will not want to double, as if he wins a single game he will have won the series.

Points of procedure

These are a few points of procedure and etiquette whose observance will make for an amiable game:

1. Shake the dice well, with your palm over the cup.
2. Let the dice fall into the right-hand half of the board. If either die does not settle completely flat in the appropriate area, there is an automatic re-throw.
3. Leave the dice on the board until you have made your full play. You may change your mind until you pick up your dice.
4. Move your pieces with one hand only, allowing your opponent to follow exactly what you are doing.
5. If a player has any doubt about the correctness of his opponent's move he may query it until he has made his own next throw.
6. Do not make your throw until your opponent has picked up his dice. If you throw prematurely your opponent, who may still want to think about his move, has the right to cancel yours; which may be a tiny bit embarrassing.

We promised at the beginning that you would learn to play backgammon in half an hour, and it has probably taken you that time to master the contents of this chapter. The next step is to play out a few games, either against an opponent or throwing the dice for each player. Before you begin, make sure that you have the following points in mind:

The start.   Each player throws one die at the beginning. If the first throw is a double, the cube is turned to 2. Subsequent doubles are ignored. As soon as the numbers are different, the player with the higher number plays both as his first move.

The move.   The play for each of the two dice must be made separately. You must always make the full legal move if you can. If you can make only one move it must, if possible, be the longer one.

Playing a double.   When you throw a double you make four moves, each one equal to the number thrown.

Points.   You may never alight, even in passing, on a triangle where your opponent has a point (two men or more).

Blots.   When you hit a blot (a lone man), this man is placed on the bar.

Entering from the bar.   A player who has men, or a man, on the bar must enter all of them into his opponent's home board before making any other play.

Bearing off.   You cannot bear off any man until all your men are in your home board. You may bring your last man in and bear off this or any other man in one move. When all your men are in your home board and you throw a higher number than the highest space you occupy, you must play first from the highest space you do occupy, either bearing off or moving within your board.

Gammons.   If one player bears off all his men before his opponent has borne off any, this is a gammon and the score for the game is doubled.

The doubling cube.   Either player, before throwing, may double by turning the cube and offering it to his opponent. If the double (or redouble) is accepted, only the player who has charge of the cube may offer the next double. If beavers are played, a player who redoubles *immediately* may keep possession of the cube.

CHAPTER TWO

The Opening Move

Although two dice can be thrown in 36 ways (6 × 6), there are only 15 possible opening moves. How so? Well, 6 of the 36 are doubles, and doubles do not occur on the opening move. As for the remaining 30, reflect that a 5 from one die and a 3 from the other is the same in effect as 3 from the first and 5 from the second. So you halve the 30 and arrive at the figure of 15.

The best first moves with various dice have been the subject of much analysis and argument over the years, and there are still different opinions about many of them. We are going to look at all the likely moves, not because it will usually make much difference which you choose but because you will pick up many ideas about the strategy of backgammon; in particular, about the way in which chances are estimated in advance.

At the end of this chapter we will list the moves in numerical order for ease of reference, but for the present we will tackle them in a logical order. In our philosophy of the game the opening moves can be divided into four groups:

1. *Pointers:* 3–1, 6–1, 4–2.

2. *Builders:* 3–2, 4–3, 5–2, 5–4, 4–1, 5–3.

3. *Six-shooters:* 6–5, 6–4, 6–3.

4. *Tempters:* 5–1, 6–2, 2–1.

1 Pointers
3–1, 6–1, 4–2

These three rolls are both advantageous and non-controversial. They enable you to make a point (establish two men) in the critical area—between 4 and 7 in your front board.

The 3–1 move

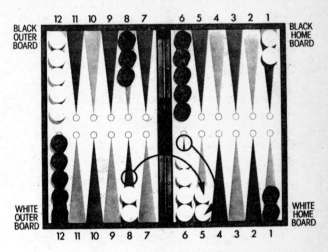

Diagram 9

White makes his 5 point, playing the 3 from W 8 to W 5, the 1 from W 6 to W 5.* To make the 5 point, beginning a block against the opponent's back men, is always a primary objective.

---

* From now on we will abstain from this kind of explanatory comment, which some writers keep going relentlessly for five or six chapters.

The 6–1 move

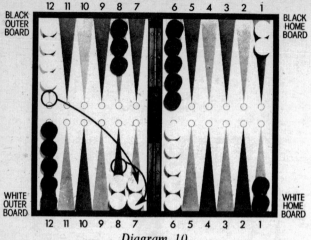

Diagram 10

By this move White establishes at once a 3-point block. Making the bar point (W 7) is especially valuable if Black throws an early 6–6 (because he is prevented from moving his two back men from W 1 to W 7).

The 4–2 move

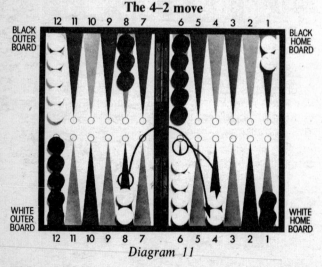

Diagram 11

The 4 point is not, at first, as valuable as the 5 point, but this is a good throw and certainly there is no better way to play it.

26

2 Builders
3–2, 4–3, 5–2, 5–4, 4–1, 5–3

We describe as 'builders' those moves that bring one or more unsupported men into the outer board. They can be hit by a long shot from W 1, but this won't be a calamity. Meanwhile you are bringing a man into, or within range of, the critical area we have been discussing. There is an excellent chance that if the blot in the outer board is not immediately hit you will be able to convert it into a valuable point, either where it stands or further forward.

The 3–2 move

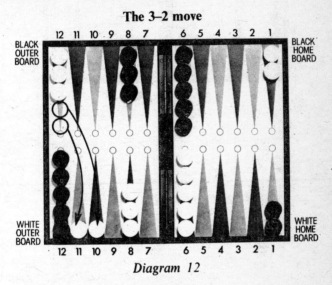

Diagram 12

The two men on W 11 and W 10 are comparatively safe from attack and are in a handy position to make any number of good points on the next throw. For example, with 2–1 you could make the 9 point, with 6–4, 4–1 or 4–3 the bar point, with 6–1 or 5–1 the 5 point, with 6–2 the 4 point. With 3–1 or 6–3 you could make either the bar point or the 5 point.

The only fair alternative to the move we suggest is to play the 2 'round the corner' as before and the 3 at the back, from B 1 to B 4. Advancing a back man to B 4 or B 5 has certain merits, as we shall see when we discuss the play in Chapter 4.

The 4–3 move

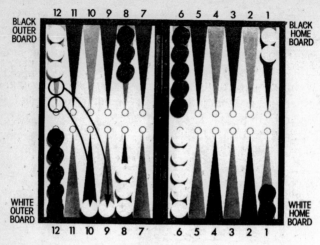

Diagram 13

The strategical object of this move is the same as for 3–2: if not hit immediately, you are a strong favourite to make a good point on the next roll. As the board stands, every throw except 5–5 will enable you to make either the bar point, the 5 point, or the 4 point.

As the men on W 10 and W 9 are somewhat more exposed than in the 3–2 move, when you went to W 10 and W 11, there is a better case now for the alternative of moving one man round the corner and one at the back: either B 12 to W 9 and B 1 to B 4, or B 12 to W 10 and B 1 to B 5.

The 5–2 move

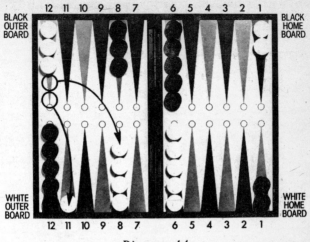

Diagram 14

The only move that can be considered for the 5 is from B 12 to W 8—not that it is strong, but because the alternative, W 8 to W 3, is worse. The man on W 11 is exposed only to 6–4 and is well placed to unite with another piece to make the bar point or the 5 point.

To play the 2 move at the back, from B 1 to B 3, is undesirable for two reasons. First, it would leave you with a lifeless position in front. Secondly, the split to B 3 has the disadvantage that an opponent who threw 5–5 or 5–3 would be able to point on the blot, transforming a moderate roll into a good one; and 3–3, always a good roll, would be stronger than ever.

The 5–4 move

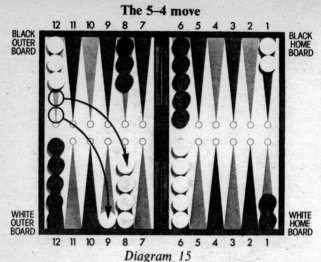

Diagram 15

This is the only constructive way to play the move, in
line with the general policy of preparing to make points
in the vital area.

To make the 4 move at the back would leave you with everything to
do in the front board. The running move from B 1 to B 10 is seldom
played with this roll.

The 4–1 move

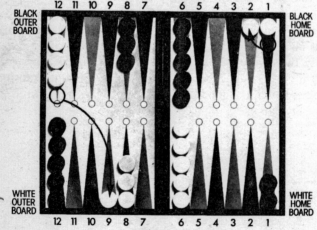

Diagram 16

White plays the 4 as a builder and splits the back men
with the 1. The split from B 1 to B 2 is not so innocuous
as it may appear.

30

The move from B 1 to B 2 does not look dynamic, but it contains some hidden power. First, it becomes more dangerous for Black to leave a blot anywhere in his front board. Suppose, for example, that after White has split his back men Black throws 5–3 or 3–2; it is risky for him to make the standard plays into his outer board, because White will have many more chances to hit him, firing from two stations.

Secondly, if White himself, after the move from B 1 to B 2, throws 4–3 or 3–2 he will be able to make the 5 point or the 4 point in his opponent's board; this is a strong play, as we explain in Chapter 4.

Thirdly, it wouldn't pay Black to hit either of the men on B 1 or B 2; he would be sending it back only one or two spaces, he might be hit in turn when White came off the bar, and, worst of all, the man left on B 1 or B 2 would play little part in the game for some time.

An alternative way of playing the 1 is to slot on the 5 point. (To 'slot' is to drop a man on an empty point, hoping to cover it later.) Black would be able to hit one or other of the blots with 19* shots out of 36, 2–2 and 4–4 hitting both, but many favourable developments are possible.

The 5–3 move

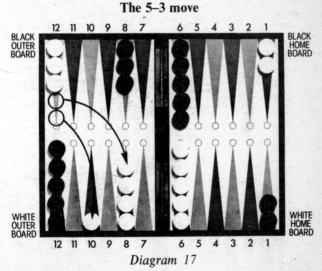

Diagram 17

As with 5–2 and 5–4, we play the 5 to W 8 and bring a builder into the outer board.

---

* When counting throws, remember always that a double is one throw, but any other roll is two throws. Thus 1–3 and 3–1 are two possible throws, although the end product is the same.

There are at least two other ways of playing this roll. A modern gambit is to run from the midpoint to W 5. As will shortly appear, we recommend a move of that type with 6–2, but with 6–2 the alternatives are not so good.

The other possibility is to make the 3 point. However, the 3 point is not of much value until the player has made higher points in the same area.

3 Six-shooters
6–5, 6–4, 6–3

A 6, considered on its own, is not a good throw at the beginning of the game. Whether you play it from B 1 to B 7 or from B 12 to W 7, it will be exposed to a 6 in return, and the opponent can throw a 6 (singly or in combination) in no fewer than 17 ways out of 36. One way of avoiding a return hit, at any rate with 6–5, is to play a long move from the back.

The 6–5 move

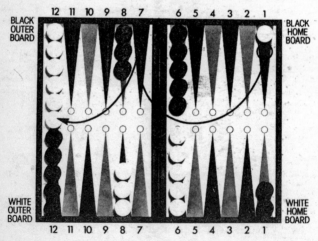

Diagram 18

This is the traditional move, taking a back man to safety on the midpoint.

The long run with 6–5 (Moscow to Vladivostock) is described by some writers as one of the best opening moves in the game. It might be more accurate to say that it was the best move with this particular throw. This more aggressive play has its supporters:

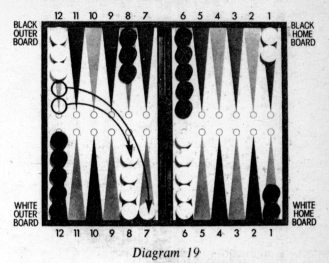

Diagram 19

The blot left by White on his bar point can be hit in 17 ways, some of which would be good rolls for Black in any event. If White can escape being hit he has made a good start towards building his front board.

This move is a calculated risk. If White is not hit he can cover the blot on his next turn with any direct 6 or 1 (20 throws) and also with 4–2, 3–3 and 2–2.

33

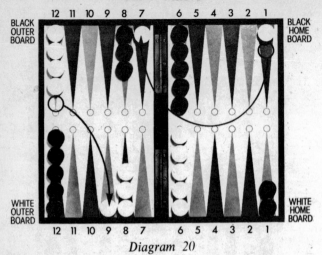

Diagram 20

White brings a builder into his outer board and plays the 6 to his opponent's bar point. The man on B 7 will often be hit, but there are several chances of a good return shot from the bar.

The opening move with 6–4 is one of the most variable plays in the game. The move shown is a little deceptive. The blot on B 7 is exposed to any 6 or 1 and the piece does not appear to be capable of achieving much where it stands. However, if Black hits, White has many chances of a successful return shot from the bar. Any 7 roll will hit, plus any safe entry combined with a 6; also 3–3 and 2–2, for a total of 16 shots. Should Black fail to hit, White may be able to bring up the other back man and make his opponent's bar point.

Many players invariably play 6–4 as a running move from B 1 to B 11 (Moscow to Nijninovgorod). The blot on B 11 is exposed to a 2 but if not hit may combine to make a point in White's outer board.

Another way to play the roll is to move from the midpoint to the bar point and split at the back from B 1 to B 5. We analyze a similar move under 6–3 below.

Finally, one writer recommends playing both men into the front board, the 4 to W 9 and the 6 to W 7. This move is full of Eastern Promise—unless the executioner gets there first. White is exposed to 20 shots, of which three hit both men.

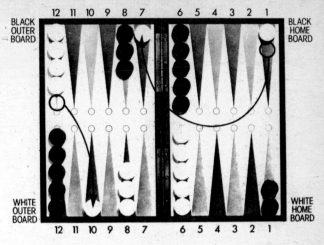

Diagram 21

This is the same move as for 6–4, except that the builder is brought to W 10 instead of W 9. The man on the bar point is at risk, but there are compensations.

The possible plays with 6–3 are much the same as with 6–4. We described under 6–4 the virtues of the move to Black's bar point. Some players favour the running move from B 1 to B 10 (Omsk to Tomsk).

An alternative move often leads to exciting play:

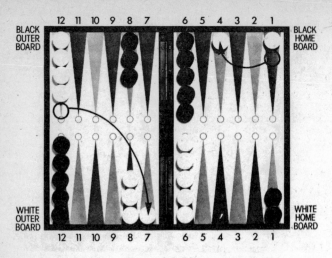

Diagram 22

This move contains threats on both sides of the board. If the man on the White bar point escapes being hit, White will have 24 ways of covering the blot.

The man on the bar point is exposed to any 6, but as before there are compensations. When White comes in from the bar he will have many chances to establish a forward point at B 4 or B 5; and if he throws any 6 except 6–6 he will be able to enter and at the same time hit the blot that Black will usually have left on W 7.

White may also bring two men into his front board at W 10 and W 7; this is risky, but there is a case for attacking moves at the start of the game.

4 Tempters
5–1, 6–2, 2–1

The first player sometimes has to choose between a move that is fairly safe but unenterprising and one that is more aggressive but risks a setback. With the three rolls in this section we prefer, though narrowly in two cases, the attacking play. Putting a bold face on it, we describe these moves as 'tempters'.

The 5–1 move

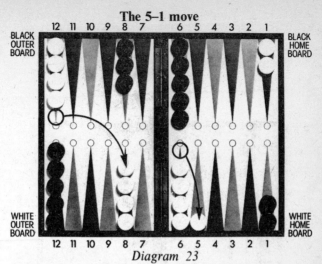

Diagram 23

Taking a chance, you slot on W 5, hoping to make the
5 point if this man is not immediately hit.

The standard alternative with the 1 is to split the back men, a play
we examined under 4–1. Another way to play this admittedly poor
roll is to move a back man to B 7 and let the opponent do his worst.

The 6–2 move

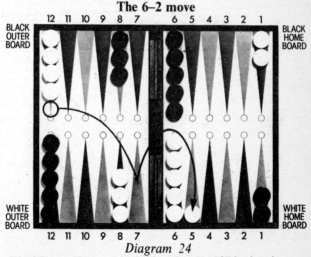

Diagram 24

The blot on W 5 can be hit in 15 ways. If Black misses—
and if White is able to cover the blot quickly—a poor
opening roll may yet turn out to the first player's
advantage.

This move is in the modern style. White is perhaps more likely to emerge with an equal game if he plays to B 7 and W 11 (compare the similar moves with 6–3 and 6–4). Another bold way to play the roll is to move from the midpoint to W 11 and W 7.

The 2–1 move

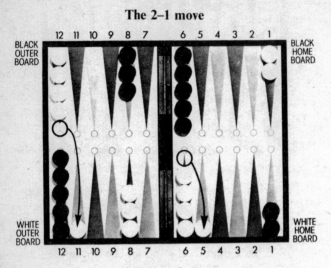

Diagram 25

If the blot on W 5 is not hit, White will be able to cover it with any 6, 3 or 1, plus 4–2, 4–4 and 2–2, a total of 31 throws. A sound alternative is to play the 2 as shown and to split the back men.

The case for the bold move is not so strong as with 5–1, because the man on W 11 is at least a start towards building a front board.

Table of Opening Moves

We list first the move illustrated above. When there is a fair alternative, we mention that as well.

6–5: Run a back man to B 12. *Alternative:* move from the midpoint to W 8 and W 7.

6–4: Play a back man to B 7 and the 4 from B 12 to W 9. *Alternatives:* play the 6 from the midpoint to the White bar point and the 4 from B 1 to B 5; or run from B 1 to B 11.

6–3: Play a back man to B 7 and the 3 from B 12 to W 10. *Alternatives:* play the 6 from the midpoint to the White bar point and the 3 either from B 1 to B 4 or from B 12 to W 10; or run from B 1 to B 10.

6–2: Run from the midpoint and slot at W 5. *Alternatives:* play a back man to B 7 and the 2 from B 12 to W 11; or play from the midpoint to the White bar point and to W 11.

6–1: Make the White bar point.

5–4: Bring a builder to W 9 and a reinforcement to W 8.

5–3: Bring a builder to W 10 and a reinforcement to W 8. *Alternatives:* make the 3 point; or run from the midpoint and slot on W 5.

5–2: Bring a builder to W 11 and a reinforcement to W 8.

5–1: Bring a reinforcement to W 8 and slot on W 5. *Alternatives:* make the 1 move at the back; or run a back man to B 7.

4–3: Bring builders to W 10 and W 9. *Alternatives:* move to W 10 and B 5, or to W 9 and B 4.

4–2: Make the 4 point.

4–1: Bring a builder to W 9 and split the back men. *Alternative:* slot on W 5.

3–2: Bring builders to W 11 and W 10. *Alternative:* play the 3 at the back, from B 1 to B 4.

3–1: Make the 5 point.

2–1: Bring a builder to W 11 and slot on W 5. *Alternative:* make the 1 move at the back.

CHAPTER THREE

Odds That Matter

It may seem natural to proceed from the opening move to the first reply, but it is difficult to get far in backgammon without referring to odds. Indeed, we have already done so. For example, we remarked in the last chapter that when a man was 6 spaces away he could be hit by 17 of the possible 36 throws. As figures of this kind have a bearing on almost every play, it seems sensible to explain right away the odds that matter.

Some people, we know, have a mental block where odds are concerned. To those we say, read this chapter nevertheless; it gives rise to many important conclusions that are not expressed in figures.

The basic odds in backgammon are extremely simple. A player must know the answers to these three questions:

1. *What are the chances of hitting a man which is from 1 to 12 spaces away?*
2. *What are the chances of throwing one or more specific numbers?*
3. *How long will it take to bear off the remaining men from various positions in the home board?*

The last question is the only one that may be difficult. And we have good news for you: we are not going to consider those odds until a later chapter.

Note, first, that questions 1 and 2 are not the same. It is one thing to hit a man which is 6 spaces away (a travelling shot), another to throw precisely a 6 (a direct shot). The first question is of the greater practical importance.

1 What are the chances of hitting a man which is from 1 to 12 spaces away?

We could set out a table expressing the chances and leave you to remember it, but it's much better, as mathematics masters used to say, to 'show the working'.

As a starting-point, there are 36 possible throws and 11 ways of throwing a specific number. Check it if you like. Say that you want to throw a 4; the possibilities are 4–1, 1–4, 4–2, 2–4, 4–3, 3–4, 4–5, 5–4, 4–6, 6–4 and double 4; two throws with each other number and one double, total 11. If a blot is next door, only a direct 1 will serve. We will start from that position and edge away.

List of travelling shots

1 space away: you can hit only with a 1. That is 11 shots out of 36, about 9 to 4 against.

2 spaces away: any 2 plus 1–1; 12 shots, 2 to 1 against.

3 spaces away: any 3 plus 2–1 (and, of course 1–2) and 1–1; 14 shots, about 13 to 8 against.

4 spaces away: any 4 plus 3–1, 2–2 and 1–1; 15 shots, 7 to 5 against.

5 spaces away: any 5 plus 4–1 and 3–2; again 15 shots, 7 to 5 against.

6 spaces away: any 6 plus 5–1, 4–2, 3–3 and 2–2; 17 shots, about 11 to 10 against.

From this point onwards the chances decline sharply because you cannot hit 7 or more with a direct shot and need instead a combination shot.

7 spaces away: 6–1, 5–2 and 4–3; 6 shots, 5 to 1 against.

8 spaces away: 6–2, 5–3, 4–4 and 2–2; 6 shots, 5 to 1 against.

9 spaces away: 6–3, 5–4 and 3–3; 5 shots, just over 6 to 1 against.

10 spaces away: 6–4 and 5–5; 3 shots, 11 to 1 against.

11 spaces away: 6–5 only; 2 shots, 17 to 1 against.

12 spaces away: 6–6, 4–4 and 3–3; 3 shots, 11 to 1 against.

You can also hit, with the aid of high doubles, at 15, 16, 18, 20 and (playing from the bar) 24 spaces away, but these are all 35 to 1 chances, which seldom come into consideration at the table.

Here are the conclusions in tabular form:

Spaces away:	1	2	3	4	5	6	7	8	9	10	11	12
Ways of hitting:	11	12	14	15	15	17	6	6	5	3	2	3

Effect of intervening points

Intervening points held by an opponent may make a difference to the chances, but not as a rule a big difference. It depends on where they are and it is easy to work out any change in the odds. Suppose, for example, that you hope to hit a man 6 spaces away and there are points at 2 and 4 on your journey: this will cut out 4–2 and 2–2, reducing the number of successful throws from 17 to 14; but if you are aiming at a man 5 spaces away, points on the same 2 and 4 will make no difference at all—you can still play 3–2 and 1–4.

Minimizing the chance of being hit

We have spoken of 'chances of hitting', but one is usually more concerned with chances of *not* being hit. Two conclusions of great practical importance can be drawn from the table above:

(a) You have a much better chance of avoiding the axe if you can stay outside the range of a direct shot (1 to 6).

(b) If you cannot avoid coming within the range of a direct shot, move up as close as you can. The best position is 1 space away, the worst 6 away. There is no difference between 4 and 5.

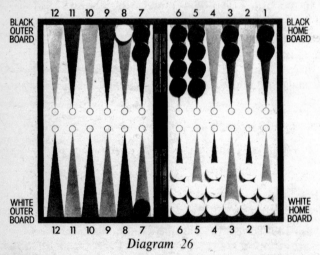

Diagram 26

White is ahead as he has 14 men in his home board against Black's 12, and White's men are also better distributed for bearing off. However, White still has to bring in the man on B 8, which is 10 spaces away from Black's man on W 7.

If Black could hit the White man on its way round, the balance of the game would change. So it is important for White to escape the attentions of the man on W 7.

(a) White throws 6–3. As he has no 6 to play in his home board, the play to W 11 is forced. Having arrived there, this man should press on to W 8. It is better to be 1 space away than 3.

(b) White throws 4–3. He could make both moves in his home board, but there is a tactical disadvantage in that. Black will also lay back with his man on W 7, retaining his best chance for a hit. While Black is bringing in the two men from his bar point and improving his home board by spreading the men more evenly, White may run out of high moves and be forced to bring his outside man within range of a direct shot. Although to be 7 spaces away would expose him to more shots than to stay 10 away, White should advance to B 11 and play the 4 in his home board. Black may continue to lay back, but if White can get a fair-sized throw on his next turn he will enter his home board with a big lead.

(c) White throws 5–4. He could make both moves within his home board, but again this would only postpone the crisis and Black would benefit. White should grasp the nettle and move to W 8.

(d) White throws 2–2. He can afford to hold back for one round. Best is to advance from B 8 to B 10 and make the remaining moves in his home board.

2 What are the chances of throwing one or more specific numbers?

This question is always relevant when a player exposes a blot. It is also important when he wants to come in from the bar, and it is convenient to examine it from that angle.

When five points are covered, the man on the bar is aiming at a single space and that, as we know, is a 9 to 4 chance. Here four points are covered*:

* For simplicity, we have left the available spaces empty. The chances would be the same, of course, if White had pieces there or Black a single piece.

43

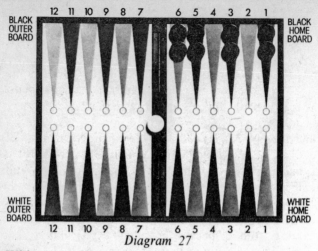

BLACK
OUTER
BOARD

BLACK
HOME
BOARD

WHITE
OUTER
BOARD

WHITE
HOME
BOARD

12 11 10 9 8 7   6 5 4 3 2 1

Diagram 27

White can come in with a 2 or a 4. Throwing two dice,
the odds are slightly in his favour.

You might think that White could enter with 11 shots on the 2 and
11 on the 4, a total of 22. That is not quite right, because you cannot
count 2–4 and 4–2 for each column. The answer is 20 shots. This makes
you 5 to 4 on—rather better odds than you might imagine. (It means
also that when you leave two blots open to direct shots it is 5 to 4
on your opponent hitting one of them directly; and there will generally
be some travelling shots as well.)

Here Black has three points covered:

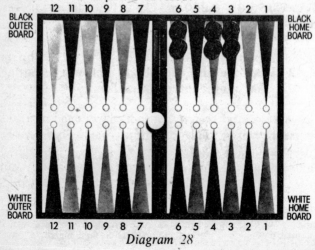

12 11 10 9 8 7   6 5 4 3 2 1

BLACK
OUTER
BOARD

BLACK
HOME
BOARD

WHITE
OUTER
BOARD

WHITE
HOME
BOARD

12 11 10 9 8 7   6 5 4 3 2 1

Diagram 28

Now White can enter with 27 shots out of 36. He is 3 to 1 on.

Betting men will see a very simple way of arriving at the figure of 3 to 1 on. With one die you would have an even chance to enter; throwing two dice, you want one of two even chances, which is 3 to 1 on. The same type of calculation can be applied to all these situations.

When only two points are covered you are a good favourite to come in.

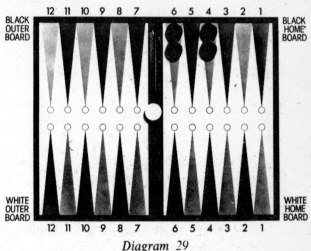

Diagram 29

White will fail to enter only with 6–4, 4–6, 6–6 and 4–4. He comes in with 32 shots, fails with 4, which makes him 8 to 1 on.

Finally, if only one point is occupied, you can miss only by throwing a double of that number; you are 35 to 1 in favour of getting on.

These are the chances in tabular form:

Chances of entering one man from the bar

Points covered	Successful throws	Odds
5	11	9 to 4 against
4	20	5 to 4 on
3	27	3 to 1 on
2	32	8 to 1 on
1	35	35 to 1 on

A player will often have two (or more) men on the bar. The odds about entering *one* of these are the same as when there is just one man on the bar. The chances of bringing in *two* men with the same throw are as follows:

Chances of entering two men from the bar

Points covered	Successful throws	Odds
5	1	35 to 1 against
4	4	8 to 1 against
3	9	3 to 1 against
2	16	5 to 4 against
1	25	9 to 4 on

This table is not as important as the other, but it is necessary to have the feel of it at least.

To enter three or four men you need a double, obviously, corresponding to an empty space.

The thought may have occurred to you: 'What is the advantage of knowing these odds? If you are on the bar you make your throw and either you come in or you don't'.

The answer to this is that you cannot plan an intelligent strategy unless you can estimate the likely outcome of an individual move. Often you will have to decide whether to hit a man or make some other play; or, looking at it from the other side, you may want to assess the risk of exposing one of your men to a hit. You then need to know, how great is the danger of being hit, and how difficult will it be to come in from the bar?

On the whole, players tend to underestimate the chances of entering from the bar. With four points covered they are mildly aggrieved when the opponent comes in with his first throw, although, as we have seen, the odds are 5 to 4 in favour. Even when five points are covered it is slightly better than evens that two throws will bring him in.*

---

* Some very good backgammon players will tell you that they know absolutely nothing about odds. You will encounter the same left-handed boast among poker players. Don't be misled. These players, from many years of experience in a limited field, play very well to the odds even if they do not, in a verbal sense, know them.

CHAPTER FOUR

The First Reply

The first reply differs from the opening move in two important respects: your opponent has made a move and this will affect your strategy in various ways; and the six doubles are at your disposal, should you be lucky enough to roll one of them.

It would be possible to give an interminable list—and it would be interminable—of opening moves and sound replies; but it is much better that you should understand the tactical aims of the second player. These are:

1. *Make a critical point*, preparing to block the opponent's back men.
2. *Hit a blot*, causing the opponent to lose time and space.
3. *Bring a builder into a favourable position*, preparing to make a good point at the next turn.
4. *Take care of his own back men*, either with a long move or by splitting them and so increasing their range.

Let us examine these aims in turn and see how they can be put into operation by various rolls. We will assume that Black has made the first move, so you continue to play from the White position.

1 Making a critical point

The critical points, in order of preference, are: your own 5 point; your own bar point; your opponent's 5 point; your opponent's bar point; and the two 4 points are not to be despised.

The throws that enable you to make the strongest of these points are 3–1, 6–1, 1–1, 3–3, 4–4 and 6–6. You will also sometimes make points effectively with 2–2, 4–2, 5–3 and 5–5, so we will look at those rolls as well in the present section.

3–1. Make your 5 point, as with the opening move. A possible exception occurs when Black has dropped a man on his 5 point.

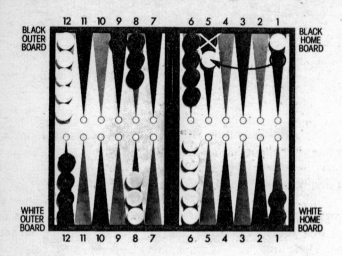

Diagram 30

Black has rolled 4–1 and has played to B 9 and B 5. White in reply rolls 3–1. Some players would make the 5 point as usual, others would hit the blot.

By hitting the blot, White accomplishes four objects: he spoils Black's plan to make this point; he threatens to make it himself (or, with 6–2, to make the bar point); he threatens the builder that Black has brought to B 9; and he forces Black to consume part of his next move in coming off the bar, perhaps breaking up what would otherwise have been a fine roll for him. (Note that, coming off the bar, Black cannot point on your blot unless he throws 4–4, 3–3 or 1–1.)

6–1. Make the bar point, as with the opening move. The only exception would be if Black had played an opening throw of 6–4 to B 7 and W 5; in that case we would hit both blots.

48

Now, for ease of reference, we will take all the doubles in succession.

1–1. This is always a good roll, enabling White to make his bar point and his 5 point.

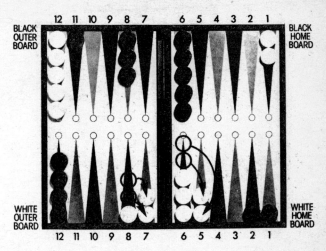

Diagram 31

White's move, in answer to Black's opening 2–1, creates a 3-point block.

Black's opening move on this occasion has made White's reply less strong than usual. Having split his back men, Black can hit the blot on W 8 with a direct 6, plus 5–1, 4–2, 5–2 and 4–3, a total of 19 rolls. If Black gets that shot he will be back in the game, but if he doesn't, and you are soon able to cover your blot, your advantage will be considerable.

2–2. Unless there are special considerations, the standard way to play this roll is to make the 11 point and the 4 point.

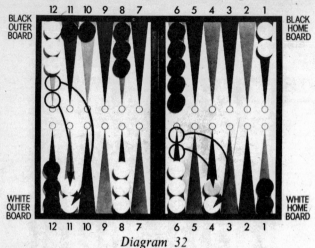

Diagram 32

Black has opened with 3–2 and White has rolled 2–2. The move shown, making two good points, is stronger than devoting the entire roll to making the Black 5 point.

However, 2–2 is a versatile throw and against certain openings by Black there are better replies than making the 11 and 4 points. Briefly, if Black has made his bar point, counter the threat of being shut in by moving the two back men to occupy Black's 5 point. If Black has left a blot on your bar point, hit it with three of your 2s and play the other to W 11. If Black has slotted on his 5 point, hit the blot and make your own 4 point. (This is stronger than the more obvious move of pointing on his blot; your two back men will exert considerable pressure on Black's board and meanwhile you have made progress in your own board.)

We have not given diagrams to illustrate these occasional situations, but set them up on your board and note what we say about the different moves; that will give you a sense of position and be far more useful than attempting to memorize them.

3–3. With this roll you have an *embarras de richesse*. You could make your bar point or your opponent's bar point, both very satisfactory moves. But even stronger, if Black's opening move has not created

50

any special conditions, is to establish three points in your home board. Here Black has opened with 5–3.

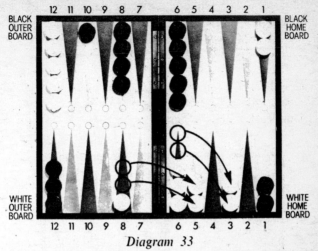

Diagram 33

White's move hems in his opponent's back men and the three points in the home board will be a menace to Black whenever he has a man on the bar. White's blot on W 8 can be hit only by 6–1 or 4–3.

White has alternative, and very good, replies to various opening moves by Black. Suppose, first, that Black, with an opening such as 2–1, has split his back men. If White were then to play 3–3 as shown above, the man on W 8 would be vulnerable to a direct 6 plus 5–1, 4–2 and 4–3. We would prefer, therefore, to make our own bar point. We would still have a 3-point block, and one feature of the position would be that Black would not be able to run with 6–5; this would now be a poor roll for him.

Some other possibilities:

Black has made his 5-point or his bar point. In this case move the two back men to B 4, to avoid being shut in. This move to B 4 is strong, whatever the circumstances.

Black has left a blot on our bar point. Hit it, making the point.

Black has left a blot on his own bar point. To hit it and make the point would give you the better position, to be sure; but to hit with one back man and make your own 5 point is a move with a little more 'class' to it. (Compare the similar move with 2–2 and the comment made there.)

51

Black has made a running move to W 10. Point on it and make your 5 point as well.

You will note two principles underlying the moves we have been looking at: generally hit a blot (other than one tucked away at W 1 or W 2); and when effective moves are presented in different parts of the board, diversify.

4–4. Again, there is a tempting choice. To make the opponent's 5 point is always strong. The other popular move is to play two men from the midpoint to the 5 point.

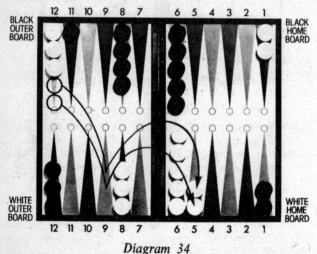

Diagram 34

Black has opened with 5–2 and White has rolled 4–4. The special strength of the diagram move is that White has made his 5 point without using any men from W 8 or W 6; these are poised to make further points in the home board.

Certain openings by Black demand a different response, the arguments being much the same as for 2–2. Thus if Black has thrown 6–1 and made his bar point, White must look to his defences. He could run to B 9 with both back men, but to make Black's 5 point and his own 9 point is somewhat better. This last point may serve as a valuable stepping-stone when White eventually brings his back men round. It is certainly better to make the 9 point than to rape the 8 point to make the 4 point.

As on the previous occasions, White should generally hit any blot that has been left on a sensitive point. If Black has dropped a man on B 5, White is happy to point there and to make his own 4 point. If Black, with a boldly played 4–1, has left blots on B 9 and B 5, White's best move is to hit both blots with a back man and, on this occasion, to make the 4 point. Black, with two men on the bar, won't be able to do much damage (only 2–2 enables him to pick up the blot on B 9, from W 12) and White will have plenty of time to take care of the blots he has left at B 9 and W 8.

5–5. Unlike the other doubles, this is not a good throw. As a rule, there is nothing to be done but bring two men from the midpoint to make the 3 point.

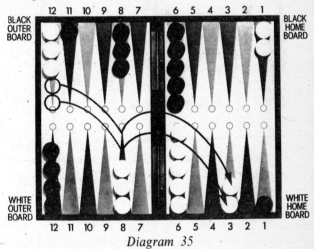

Diagram 35

Black has opened with 2–1 and has split his back men.
White's play with 5–5 is not particularly strong, but there is no good alternative.

As Black has split his back men in the example above, White has the opportunity to point on W 1, hitting the blot, and to make the 3 point as well. The objection to this is that the men on W 1 will be out of play, the outer board will be naked except for the blot on W 8, and Black will be able to move freely when he comes in from the bar.

If Black has split to White's 3 point, 5–5 becomes a good roll. White can make the same move as above with the advantage of pointing on a blot; or, more dynamic, he can play from W 8 and W 6, pointing on W 3 and W 1 and putting two men on the bar. It will probably take Black at least two throws to bring both men in, so White will have time to amend the deficiencies in his outer board.

6–6. Unless Black has made his bar point with 6–1 you will make both bar points and be well away. So let's look at the worst that can happen:

Diagram 36

Black has opened with 6–1, spoiling White's normal move with 6–6. The move shown is better than making the bar point and the 2 point, which would weaken W 8 and leave two men out of play.

If the blot on W 2 is hit later on, we can be philosophical about it. When it comes round again this man may bring much needed support to our midfield area.

4–2. When nothing better is offered we can always make the 4 point, as on the opening move. But if Black has left a blot on any sensitive point we hit it, using the full throw if necessary.

5–3. Normally play this as you would on the opening move, bringing builders to W 10 and W 8. If Black has left a blot on B 9, hit it with a back man. Make the 3 point in only two circumstances: when Black has obligingly left a blot on W 3; or when a builder on W 10 would be exposed to a direct shot, Black having moved a back man to W 4 or beyond.

2 Hitting a blot

The remaining 11 plays (22 rolls) are not strong in themselves, but they improve if you can hit a blot. Take this situation:

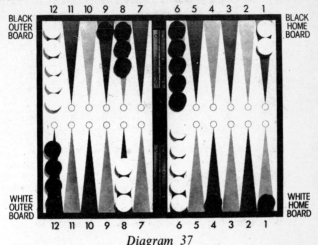

Diagram 37

Black has played an opening 4–3 by moving a builder to B 9 and advancing a back man to W 4.

White throws 5–2. He should play the 5 to W 8 and hit the blot on W 4 with the 2. It is true that this exposes him to several return shots, but he cannot ignore the challenge. It won't be fatal if he is hit at this early stage, and if he escapes he will have numerous chances to establish a strong position. (There is another, more sophisticated, way to play the roll: hit on W 1 and play the 2 from B 1 to B 3, threatening the blot on B 9.)

White throws 3–2. He cannot consider bringing in two builders while his outer board is threatened by two men. Also, if Black's man on W 4 is not removed he may succeed in making a point at W 4 or W 5, driving a wedge into White's home board. Although it places a man temporarily out of play on W 1, White's best play is to hit on W 4 and continue with the same man to hit on W 1. His board won't look strong after this, but remember that Black may have to expend the whole of his next move in coming off the bar—and perhaps two moves.

In the next example White hits in his home corner for a rather different reason.

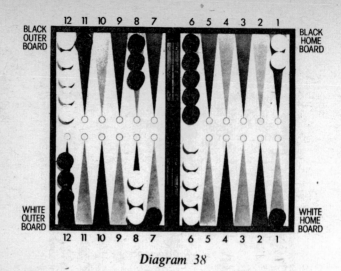

Diagram 38

Black has thrown 6–2 and has moved one man to his opponent's bar point and one to B 11. In reply, White rolls 6–5.

Certainly White must hit the man on the bar point with his 6. What about the 5? Well, the piece he has brought to the bar point is exposed to 16 return shots and the best way to protect it is to hit a second man on W 1, putting two men on the bar. If Black does not at once hit the blot on W 1 White will have 24 throws to make his bar point; and if Black does hit on W 1, White won't be sorry to have this man in circulation again and will still have many chances to come in from the bar and at the same time cover the blot on W 7. This example shows the effectiveness of putting two men on the bar.

3 Bringing in a builder

When the second player cannot make a point or hit a blot and has one of the typical 'builder throws' such as 2–1, 3–2, 4–1, 4–3, 5–2, 5–4, and some 6s, he will think first of playing these throws in the same way as on the opening move. But if Black has split his back men, White may have to reconsider; he may make the usual move with 2–1; but to bring two men into the outer board, with 3–2 or 4–3, becomes too risky.

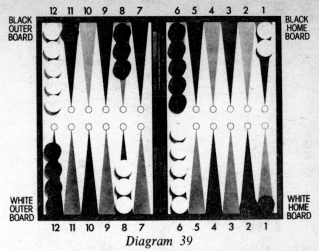

Diagram 39

Black has rolled 2–1 as his opening move and has split his back men. White has to consider the added risk of bringing builders into his outer board.

White rolls 4–3. If he brings two builders to W 9 and W 10 they will be exposed to combination shots of 7, 8 and 9, a total of 17 throws, of which a few might be put to better use elsewhere. He could avoid leaving a blot by moving from his midpoint to his 6 point, but that would achieve nothing and would give Black the initiative. Or he could move to W 9 and B 4. The man on W 9 would be exposed to 12 shots, but if this man were hit White would have several chances, when coming off the bar, to establish a forward point in Black's board. The man on B 4 would also be exposed to several shots, but Black would usually be leaving a blot in return. Another sound play would be to move to W 10 and B 5.

White rolls 6–3. After Black has split his back men, White cannot consider dropping a man on W 7 or W 4, where it would be exposed to a direct shot from two men. To run to B 10 with a back man would also be poor play, because this man would be exposed to 1s as well as 3s. The other standard move with 6–3, a back man to B 7 and a builder to W 10, would be suicidal: Black would be able to hit one man or the other with 31 shots, and with 9 of these he could make his bar point as well. The remaining possibility is to bring a builder to W 10 and hit on W 2. This is unorthodox play, but it looks quite good here. If Black comes off the bar to W 3, W 4 or W 5 and does not succeed in hitting anywhere, White will have several chances to point on the blot or to put two men on the bar.

Now let's look at a position where Black, when splitting his back men, has moved to a more advanced position in White's home board.

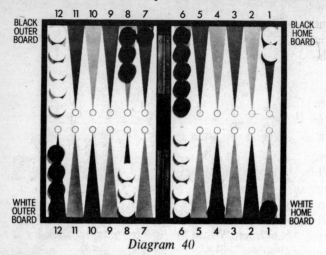

Diagram 40

Black has played an opening 6–3 in one of the less common ways, bringing a man to his bar point and splitting to the White 4 point.

White rolls 5–3. This is one of the few rolls with which White is unable to hit either of the more tempting blots. As a builder to W 10 would be within range of a direct 6, White may think of making his 3 point, which indeed would not be a mistake. Another possibility is to split the back men, moving to W 8 and B 4; the objection to this is that Black will have many chances to point on the blot at B 4 or to hit both blots.

Now look again at the first move—to W 8 and W 10. You will see that it is not so risky as it appeared. If Black throws a 6 and hits the blot on W 10 he may be giving up the chance to cover the blot on his bar point. This is an early introduction to the 'duplicator' theme, which we develop in Chapter 8.

4 Taking care of the back men

With the long throws (6–5 and 6–4) the second player will usually run to B 12 or B 11, if only because there won't be any sensible alternative. Moves to B 9 or B 10 are good if they hit a blot, and may be advisable if Black is threatening to form a block.

Failing a satisfactory long throw, White can extend the range of his back men, and slightly improve the chances of their escape, by splitting them within his opponent's home board. The split to B 2 is usually the best way to play a 1 at the beginning of the game; we commented on the merits of this move when describing the opening throw with 4–1 in Chapter 2. The split to B 3 has certain drawbacks, noted under 5–2 in the same chapter.

Splitting to B 4 or B 5

As between the two, the split to B 4 is slightly to be preferred because it is bad for White if his opponent is able to make his valuable 5 point and hit a blot at the same time.

The move to either point is inadvisable in two circumstances:

(a) When the opponent already has a builder in his outer board not more than six spaces away from where the forward man would be. Or:

(b) When the opponent has already made his bar point or a second point in his home board. The danger now is that one or both blots will be hit and White will be forced into a blot-hitting contest where his opponent will have the advantage.

The situation is different if White is making a hit at the same time as he makes the advance to B 4 or B 5. He need not be so apprehensive now of an opposing piece in Black's outer board.

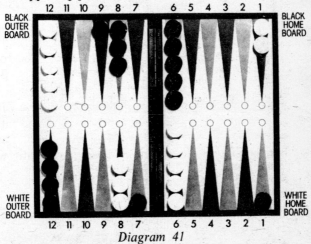

Diagram 41

Black has thrown 6–4 on his opening turn. He has brought a back man to White's bar point and a builder into his outer board.

(a) White throws 3–2. This, obviously, is a poor reply. If he brings two builders into his outer board they will be under strong threat from Black's man on W 7. Nor can White safely bring in one builder and split at the back to B 4, with men bearing on it from three stations. A feeble move from the midpoint to W 8 would leave Black with a strong initiative. The best that White can do is hit on W 1 and hope to hit again after Black has come off the bar.

(b) White throws 6–3 (or 6–4). Now White is in a fair position to hit at W 7 and split his back men. As Black has to come off the bar he won't be able to point on B 4 (or B 5) unless he throws a lucky double, nor will he be able to hit two blots. He will probably come in safely and hit one of the blots with another piece, but White will have several return shots. Suppose, for example, that Black makes the fair roll of 6–5. He will come in at W 5 and hit on W 7, leading to this position:

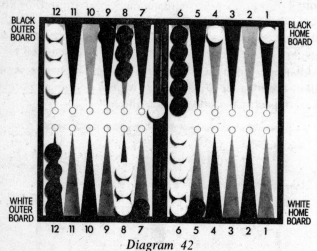

Diagram 42

Although White is on the bar he is well placed either to come in safely and hit one of the blots, or to make an advanced point in his opponent's home board, or, with certain throws, to do both.

Coming in from the bar in this position, White can make the 4 point with 20 shots (any travelling 4 plus 3–2, 5–3 and 3–3) and the 5 point with 5–1 or 5–4. With the front man on B 5 instead of B 4 he has 21 shots. A point in this area has the following advantages:

1. It prevents Black from establishing a formidable block.

2. It stands as a permanent threat against unguarded men in Black's outer board.
3. If White throws a high double his chances of escape will be much better than if he were still on B 1.
4. The forward point will provide a safe landing-place for White when at any time he is put on the bar. The effect of this is that White need not be unduly nervous of leaving blots; he can make aggressive moves with less than the usual risk.

It is prudent to add that the value of these forward points diminishes as the game progresses. Once the stage of bringing in has been reached, one of the two back points is much more of a threat to the opponent than one of the front points.

Many of the moves we have discussed in this chapter involve quite fine points. We emphasize again that what is important is not that you should remember one move as against another, but that you should follow the argument. If you can look at the board and say, 'That would be a good move because...' or 'That would be a poor move because...', you will have made an immense stride towards becoming a good player.

CHAPTER FIVE

Bringing In and Bearing Off

Before proceeding to the uncertain area of the middle game we are going to consider the end game, where a number of standard situations arise in every game that is played to a finish.

There are two problems: how to bring the last men into the home board, and how to bear them off in the lowest number of rolls. Although bearing off comes last, it it advisable to study it first, because the technique of bearing off is a pointer to the technique of bringing in.

Bearing off falls into two parts, depending on whether or not the opponent still has one or more men back which are capable of hitting any blot you may be forced to leave. Bearing off when there is no contact is the easier and less anxious procedure.

Bearing off when there is no contact

'No contact' means that all the opponent's men are on their way home and there is a simple race to be the first to bear off all the pieces. A number of general principles can be laid down.

1 When you can bear off a man in a single move, almost always do so.

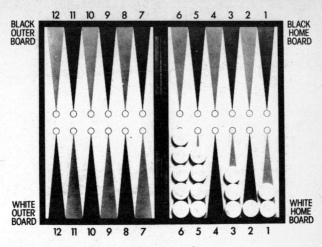

Diagram 43

This is not a good board from which to bear off, because of the vacant space on 4 and the preponderance of men on the high numbers. However, one often starts with an even worse board.

If White throws a 4 he can move down from the 6 or 5 but cannot bear off a man directly with that die. Double 4 would be particularly annoying in the sense that White wouldn't be able to remove any man at all; however, moving four men from the 6 point would much improve his future prospects.

Say that White throws 2–1. That also is a poor roll. He could improve the look of his board by moving from 6 to 4 and from 5 to 4, but he would still have fifteen men to bear off. The alternative is to take off men from 2 and 1. Quite possibly it would come to the same in the end, but the normal practice is to bear off the two men. This gives you the best chance to get off in a *few* moves, because you may have the luck to throw high numbers and not waste throws of 1 and 2.

Is it *ever* wrong to bear off a man from a direct throw? No one has devised a neat formula, but there are occasions when it looks as though a move within the board might be better. Consider this position:

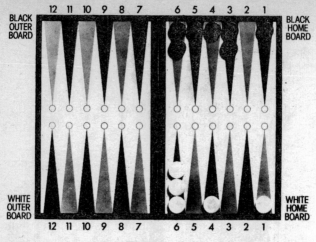

Diagram 44

White has five men left, Black has seven, and it is White's throw. As Black will normally need at least four throws to be off, White may expect to win if he can get off in three throws after his present turn.

White rolls 2–1. With the 2 he moves down from 6. What about the 1? If, following the general rule, he bears off from 1, his home board will read: 2 0 2 0 0 0 (Position A). The alternative is to make both moves from the 6 point, leaving this board: 1 1 2 0 0 1 (Position B).

We don't want to make heavy weather of this, but Position B looks slightly more promising. We are aiming to be off in three more throws, remember. Having an odd number, we can afford to miss once. With Position A we can afford to miss twice—but we may miss three times. (With 5–3, 5–2, 3–2 and 2–1 we miss twice on the first throw.)

No doubt, a computer could supply an exact answer to this little problem. There cannot be a lot in it, so you won't go far wrong if you follow the simple rule and always bear off from a direct throw.

2 When you can bear off a man with a combination move, generally do so.

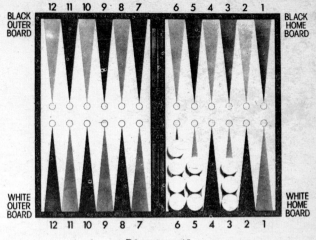

Diagram 45

With his remaining men distributed over three columns, White is sure to encounter some frustration before the finish. For the moment, however, he can bear off at least one man with any throw except 4–4.

White throws 2–1, 4–1 or 4–2. In each case he can bear off one man by a combination move, and that would be the natural play.

Despite the general principle, there is often not much to choose between bearing off a man and making two moves within the board. Towards the end it may be apparent that to move within the board would be better.

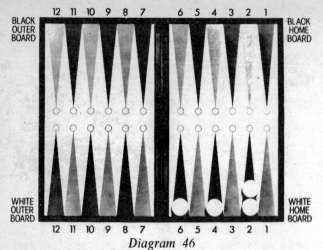

Diagram 46

With four men left, White wants to be sure of getting off in three throws. It may be better to leave four men well situated than three in awkward positions.

White throws 3–1. If he bears off from 4 he will be left with an awkward 1 0 0 0 2 0. There are many ways now of failing to get off in two throws. By moving from 6 to 3 and from 2 to 1 White leaves 0 0 1 1 1 1, a far more promising assortment.

A special situation arises when a player can see that he will probably need a double on his last turn.

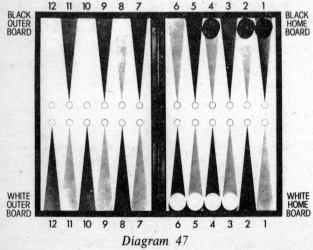

Diagram 47

As Black will surely be off in two throws at most, White will need a double either now or on his last turn.

White throws 2–1. If he bears off from 3, 5–5 will win at the finish, but not 4–4. The correct play is to bring in the outside men, from 6 to 4 and from 5 to 4; then 4–4 will be good enough.

3 When you are moving within your home board, the priorities are: (a) move down from the 6 point; (b) occupy a vacant space, evening the spread; (c) move down from the highest number.

A man on the 6 point is a liability because only a 6 will bear it off directly. If you have a man on 6 and none on 5, a 5 is a wasted shot; but if you have a man on 5 and none on 6, either a 6 or a 5 will bear this man off.

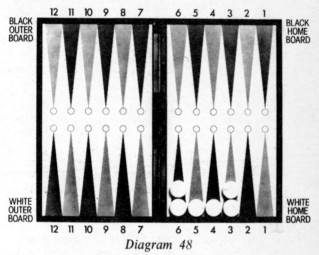

Diagram 48

Unless he throws a double, White is unlikely to be off in three rolls. The realistic aim is to be off in four throws, and the first objective is to lessen the load on the 6 point.

White throws 5–2. He can bear off a man from the 5 point and the question is what to do with the 2. The choice is between moving from 6 to 4 or from 3 to 1, so that a 1 won't be wasted. Although it leaves you with an awkward board, it is right to move down from the 6. But if you had only *one* man on 6 it would be right to even the spread.

When your highest number is a 5 the urgency to move from the high point is not so strong; it will usually be better to even the spread.

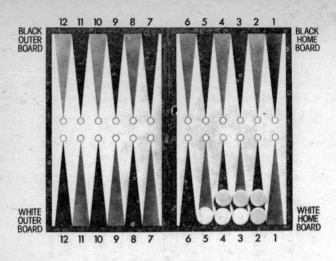

Diagram 49

In this type of situation, to fill the gap on 1 is more important than to move down from the highest number.

White rolls 4–1. The choice is between bearing off from 5 or bearing off from 4 and moving from 2 to 1. Clearly, 0 1 1 2 1 1 is a better board than 0 0 2 2 2 0, where any 1 would miss. You don't need to worry about the 5 in the first case, because it is about 10 to 1 on that you will throw a 5 *or a 6* in three rolls. It is true that throwing a 5 or 6 will not by itself see you off the board in three rolls; the point we are making is that in general you need not be afraid of having a 5 on your board. It is worth knowing that if your last two men are on 5 and 2 you have a better than even chance of bearing off in one throw, but with men on 6 and 1 or 4 and 3 a less than even chance. We say more about these odds in the chapter on the Doubling Cube.

Bearing off when there is contact

When Black still has men at the back, White's objective in most cases is not so much to bear off men quickly as to avoid leaving a blot and being hit. Thus he will often make a safe move in preference to bearing off one or two men.

68

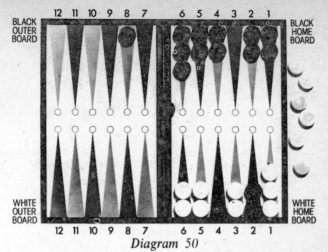

Diagram 50

White has borne off six men, but his position is still precarious. If he is hit, either from the bar or by Black men on W 2, the game may turn against him.

White rolls 5–3. As Black has a strong home board, with five points covered, it would be madness to bear off men from 5 and 3, leaving two blots. White can play safely for the moment, moving from 6 to 1 and from 6 to 3.

When there are several ways of moving safely, it is generally right to bring down from the highest number.

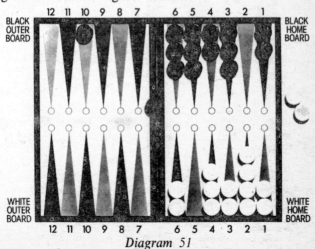

Diagram 51

White is in a strong position but cannot afford to be careless. The Black man on the bar still imposes a threat.

White rolls 4–2. He could bear off from the 4 and the 2, quite safely for the moment; but then 5–1 or 6–1 at the next turn would force him to leave a blot, and if this were hit there would be a new favourite. The safe play is to make both moves from the 6 point. There are two reasons for this: you will be in no danger of leaving a blot on the next turn; and you are happy to leave the 5 and 6 points clear for Black to come in. As soon as Black enters from the bar, your worries are over.

There are two special points to remember when bearing off under threat:

(a) *Whenever possible, avoid having three men on your highest point and precisely two on the next point.*

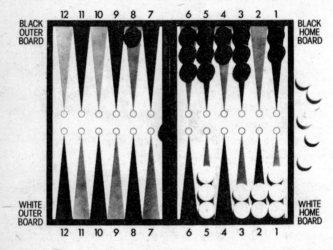

Diagram 52

Believe it or not, White is in a perilous position, because he has left himself with three men on his highest point.

White has borne off five men but now has the dreaded three men on his highest point. The gap on his 4 point is also a weakness. No fewer than 22 throws will compel him to leave a blot. Now make a small change, moving one of the three men on 5 to the 2 point. With this board only 6–1, 5–1 and 4–1 are fatal—6 throws instead of 22.

(b)   If you cannot avoid having three men on your highest point, aim to have three men on the next point also.

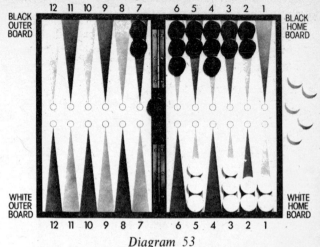

Diagram 53

This is the same board as in Diagram 52, except that one man has been transferred from the 1 point to the 3 point. White's position is far less dangerous, because he has an odd number of men on *both* his highest points.

Only a combination of 6, 5 and 4—a total of 6 shots—will force White to leave a blot now. Note that a high double will not incommode him. In general, if you can throw 6–6 and not leave a blot you can be satisfied with your move. Despite this principle, you will sometimes be unable to avoid leaving a double shot. For example, if Black holds your 1 point and you have two men on 6, two on 5, 6–5 will be a disaster. It is better, if you can, to load the high points before you begin to bear off. You will then be safe for a while and your opponent may roll a high number and be forced to run.

Bringing in

When you are bringing the last men into your home board, there are three guiding principles:

1. When the race is on, and you want to bring in your men and bear off as quickly as possible, bring them in 'economically'. That means, do not, for choice, use a long throw such as a 5 or 6 to take a man to a low point in your home board.

2. If it won't be too uneconomical in the sense described above, aim to bring men into vacant spaces. You will then be less likely to waste shots when bearing off.

3. When you have distant men in Black's outer board, aim to bring them 'round the corner'. Then you will be able to move them into your home board with a direct throw.

All three principles are illustrated in the following example:

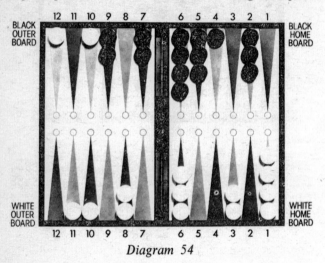

Diagram 54

Black, with only four men to bring in, and all those near home, is ahead, but the game is by no means over.

Instead of looking at complete rolls, we will consider how individual numbers should be played by White:

A Six. Bring in from W 11.

A Five. Bring in from W 10 to the vacant space on W 5.

A Four. Either bring in from W 10 or move round the corner from B 10 to W 11 or from B 12 to W 9. To move a man to the middle of the outer board is not a waste, because this man can then be brought into the home board more easily.

A Three. Either move the man on B 10 round the corner or bring in from W 8.

A Two. Bring in one of the men on W 8.

A One. Move the man on B 12 round the corner.

Moving from the outer board into the home board is essentially the same process as bearing off. Just as it is easier to bear off two men from 5 and 2 than from 6 and 1, it is easier to bring men in from W 11 and W 8 than from W 12 and W 7. The principle of 'evening the spread' applies equally to both parts of the board.

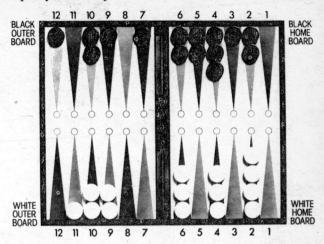

Diagram 55

The game is fairly even. White will probably be the first to begin bearing off, but at the moment his home board is not well organized.

White rolls 4–2. He should make the same moves from the outer board as from a similar position in the home board. As there is a vacant space on 5 he should play the 4 from W 9 to W 5 and the 2 from W 10 to W 8.

Good technique in bringing in and bearing off is the deciding factor in a high proportion of games. So, check all the 'headlines' in this chapter and be sure that you have them firmly in mind.

CHAPTER SIX

Who's Ahead?

After a look at the end game we return to the more complex area of the middle game. In backgammon, as in chess, the period after the opening exchanges tends to be difficult. A few blots have been hit, a few points have been made, and when things settle down a player looks at his board and wonders, now what?

Before he can begin to answer that question, he must know how he stands in a running game. That is to say, supposing no more blots were hit, would he be favourite to bear off all his men before his opponent? The question may seem academic when several pieces are still shut in, but even at this stage the answer may be some guide to tactics. Later on, there will come a time when it may be possible to avoid further contact, and then a player *must* take note of whether he is ahead, about equal, or behind. He must know for two reasons: it will affect the style of game he should adopt and it will determine whether he should double or accept an opponent's double. In this chapter we are concerned mainly with the first part of the exercise— how to assess one's position in a potential running game; in short, how to count.

To understand what is meant by counting, let us begin by examining White's position before a single move has been made.

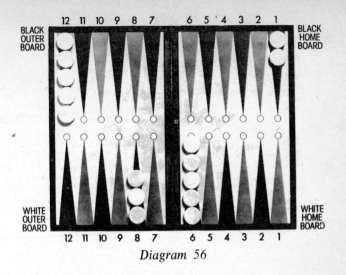

12 11 10 9 8 7   6 5 4 3 2 1

BLACK
OUTER
BOARD

BLACK
HOME
BOARD

WHITE
OUTER
BOARD

WHITE
HOME
BOARD

12 11 10 9 8 7   6 5 4 3 2 1

Diagram 56

Here you have an empty board. Throwing two dice in
the normal way, and assuming for the moment no
overlap, how many 'pips' would you need to throw,
and how many throws would you need to make, to
bear off all fifteen men?

Taking pips first, it would take 24 pips each to bear off the two back
men, a total of 48; 13 pips each to bear off the five men on the midpoint,
total 65; 8 pips each to bear off the three men on W 8, total 24; 6 pips
each to bear off the five men on W 6, total 30; grand total, 167.

The other way to count is by throws. The average throw is just over
8; dividing this into 167, you conclude that you could bear off in
between 20 and 21 throws.

These are artificial exercises, of course, designed simply to show that
there are two tests by which the relative positions of the players may
be compared. On the whole, the count by pips gives a more accurate
indication in the early and middle stages, but the count of throws is
far more significant towards the finish.

At the beginning of the game the pieces on the two sides occupy
identical positions, but after a few moves the pattern changes. So the
question arises, how, without holding up the game for too long, do
you assess the relative positions when the boards look quite different?

Broadly speaking, there are four methods:

1. The detailed count of pips.
2. The running check.
3. The count by throws.
4. The mirror method.

Some of these are more accurate than others, some are more difficult, some apply better to one sort of position than another, so we need to look at them all.

1 The detailed count of pips

At any stage of the game a player can stop and total the pips on the two sides, applying the method we described above. Professional players, in a tournament for big money, do this; but it takes a little time and is too laborious for most amateur contests. When all the men are in the home board, or close to, it doesn't take so long, of course, but at this stage it may be better to count the likely throws.

2 The running check

Some players have a good idea of the relative positions at any time of the game. They take note of any shots that make more than a minimal change. This running check is fine for anyone who can keep it up without loss of concentration.

3 The count by throws

Throws, not pips, decide the game, so there is a logical basis for estimating in terms of throws. Taking 8 as an average throw, you mentally divide the board into sections and consider how many throws you will need to bring this man round, to bear that man off, and so on, and then you apply the same test to your opponent's board. This method, as we said, is good towards the end but not very reliable in the middle of the game.

4 The mirror method

When practicable, this is the quickest way to arrive at an answer. You make a few mental adjustments so that the lay-out of your board will mirror that of your opponent. You keep count of the adjustments and you have the answer in terms of pips. This method is convenient whenever the two boards have a roughly similar pattern, as here:

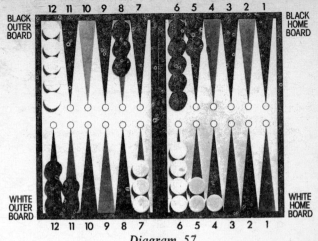

Diagram 57

It is unlikely that there will be any further contact, so it is vital to know which side is ahead in a running game.

Using the mirror method and looking first at the outer boards, we mentally transfer two Black men to the midpoint so that the five men there will reflect the five men on the opposite midpoint. It would cost Black two pips to arrive at this equality, so White stands at plus 2. The three men on B 8 can be moved one space along to mirror the White men on W 7. Again we have made Black a small gift of three pips, so White is now plus 5. Turning to the inner board, Black has one more man on his 6 point than White; mentally abolish that, and White is entitled to another six, making him plus 11. The men on the 5 point already cancel one another. White remains with a man on the 4 point. Docking him four pips for that, we subtract 4 from his lead of 11 and the conclusion is that White is 7 pips ahead.

You could get there still more quickly by noting Black's disadvantage in various sections of the board. In the home board he has a 6 as against White's 4, he is minus 2; he is three behind if you compare the 7 and 8 points, minus 5; and two behind on 11 and 12, minus 7 altogether.

Counting the pips one by one would necessarily produce the same answer. Count 65 for the White men on B 12, 21 for the three men on W 7, and so on. The totals are 124 for White, 131 for Black. The lower total is better, of course, so White is 7 ahead, as already determined.

As for throws, White might be off in fifteen rolls with average luck, Black in sixteen. Assuming it is White's turn, he has a fair lead. Does the lead justify a double? We look at this position again in Chapter 10.

Apart from the simple count, there will usually be other factors to consider. Look at this next diagram and see if you can determine who is ahead and how the game stands.

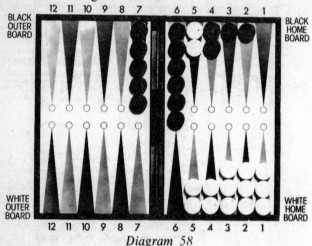

Diagram 58

White's board is well arranged for bearing off, but he has two men comparatively far back. It is not easy to see at a glance who is ahead.

With such dissimilar boards, the mirror method cannot be applied. If you count pips you will find the score is 84 for Black, 76 for White, giving White a modest lead. It is worth while looking at the throws as well. White will need, on average, about three-and-a-half throws to bring the two men on B 5 into his home board (they have, between them, 28 spaces to travel). Black cannot fail to bring in his outside men with three throws and by that time he will probably have evened up his board somewhat. But Black will still have at least six men on his 6 point and probably more by the time he has brought in the five men from his bar point. Thus although Black may be the first to begin bearing off, White should overtake him.

Another factor comes into the reckoning, however. White will not necessarily escape with both back men on his first roll. Indeed, the odds are 5 to 4 against. If he throws something like 4–2 he will have to consider whether to play safely within his home board or move out one man. If he throws 5–1 or 6–1 or 5–2 or 6–2 he will have no alternative to leaving a blot. This may not be fatal as Black has only three points covered at the moment, but it introduces an element of uncertainty. To sum up, White is slightly ahead in a running game, but this is offset by his tactical disadvantage.

When a player throws a high number such as 6–6 or 5–5 he must visualize the effect before he makes his move. Consider this example:

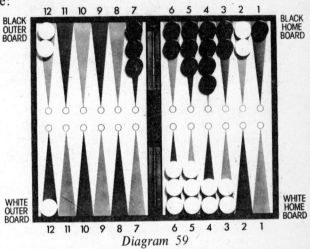

Diagram 59

White is well behind at the moment and his back men can escape only with a 6. Supposing he gets the chance to rescue both of them, should he take it?

White throws 6–6, the only move that allows him to escape with both back men. Before doing anything like that, he must consider what the position will be if he brings those two men to W 11. It is not necessary to do any counting to see that he will have no chance at all in a running game. His best hope is to leave the back men where they are and move two men from the midpoint, making the 1 point. He may well get the chance of a hit and meanwhile, with one man still on W 12 and spare men on W 6 and W 5, he has room to move without breaking up his board.

As we remarked earlier, pips are no guide at all towards the end of the game. As a simple example, suppose that White has two men on 6 (twelve pips) and Black three men on 1 (three pips): White, with the throw, is a good favourite to win.

When there are only a few men left, to have the first throw is obviously a great advantage. It is also an advantage to have an even number of men against an odd number, rather than the other way round. The point can readily be seen from this example:

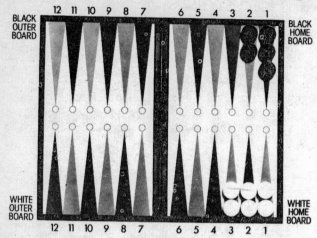

Diagram 60

White has a count of 12 against 7 and an extra man, but having the throw he is a clear favourite. He is almost sure to be off in three rolls and his opponent will need a double to beat that.

Now give White an extra man on 1 and Black an extra man on 2, so that White has seven men against his opponent's six. The position is reversed because White, failing a double, will need four throws to be off the board, while Black will surely be off in three.

As this chapter will have made clear, to judge who is ahead in a running game is a problem with no neat solution. Depending on the general position, it may help to count the pips, to count the throws, to note the possibility of contact, to compare the home boards, or to do all these things. It is not easy at first, but with a little experience the majority of situations can be summed up with fair speed and accuracy.

CHAPTER SEVEN

Racing, Containment and Control

When one of the present authors was learning the game from a player of world class, his opponent would say from time to time, 'What are you trying to do?' That is an excellent question for a backgammon player to ask himself at every stage of the game, for unless he has a basic strategy his moves will be disconnected and inefficient.

As a start, it is helpful to understand in what *type* of game you are currently engaged. It may be a running game, or a blot-hitting contest, or a game of containment and control.

Playing a running game

Until something happens, as it were, the objectives at the beginning of any game are to extricate the back men, to contain the opponent's back men, and to make speed round the board. Sometimes everything will go well at first. If you hit a few blots early on and avoid being hit back, you know without needing to count that you are well ahead. The policy then is to retain the lead, moving men into safe positions and leaving as few blots as possible. If you already have a fair lead it won't help you to hit further blots left by your opponent; that will just make it easier for him to build up a good defensive position.

The opponent, on the other hand, being behind in the race, will seek to complicate the position. He will place blots in challenging positions and will play what we describe as a game of board control. We say more about that later.

In some games there will be little or no contact. Both sides free their back men early and the few hits balance out. Such games depend largely on who throws the better dice, but you can assist your cause by keeping in mind the principles of bringing in, as described in Chapter 5.

A blot-hitting contest

More often, in the modern style of backgammon, each side will harry the other and neither will have time to build up a good board. This sort of game is known as a blot-hitting contest. The important thing here is not to get involved in what the boxing commentators call 'toe-to-toe slogging'. It is very useful, in the midst of such exchanges, to establish a forward point in the opponent's home board, and equally useful to establish a second point in your own home board. Our 'odds that matter' become quite dramatic when that second point is made. When you have only one point in your home board it is 35 to 1 on your opponent being able to enter one man from the bar, 9 to 4 on his entering two men; but when you hold two points it is 8 to 1 on his bringing in one man, 5 to 4 *against* his bringing in two men; and if he fails to enter, the move you gain will surely be useful at this stage of the game.

The moral from this is that you don't want to get into a blot-hitting contest when your opponent holds two points and you hold only one. After a few moves in which neither side has made much progress, this situation is reached:

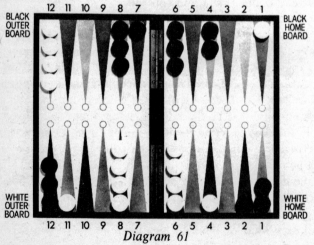

Diagram 61

The game is still in the blot-hitting stage. White is at a slight disadvantage in any such contest, as his opponent has an extra point in his home board.

White throws 5–1. The choice is between hitting the blot on Black's bar point and making the 3 point. As a rule, to hit on B 7 with the last back man is an attractive proposition, because if this man is not hit at once he may escape altogether on the next move. In this case, however, the move does not appeal, because Black is almost certain to hit some blot in return. A 4 from the bar, or any safe entry combined with a 1, 2, 3 or 6, will hit either at B 7 or W 4; and White, as we have noted above, should not wish to engage in a blot-hitting contest when he has only one point in his home board and the opponent has two. Thus, to make the 3 point is a clear choice. If Black now fails to cover the blot on B 7, White will have at least an equal game.

Containment and control

We need not dwell longer on the development of no-contact and blot-hitting games, which for the most part play themselves until a change occurs. We move now to the more common and more difficult games in which racing, containment and control all play a part. A game begins:

Black rolls 4–2 and makes his 4 point.

White rolls 6–6 and makes both bar points.

Black rolls 2–1. He brings a builder to B 11 and slots on B 5, producing this position:

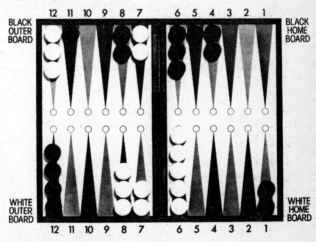

Diagram 62

Thanks to an early 6–6, White is away to a fast start. He now throws 5–4, another good roll.

White was intending in any event to run further with his back men, and the fact that he can hit as well is a bonus. He plays the 5 to his midpoint and with the 4 hits the blot on B 11.

Black comes off the bar with 5–1. This is quite a good combination: he makes his 5 point with the 1 and is happy to slot on W 5. This sort of move, especially when backed up by the point on W 1, is a modest essay in board control. Black would be happy to make the White 5 point and, failing that, his man on W 5 exerts some pressure on White's outer board. The position is:

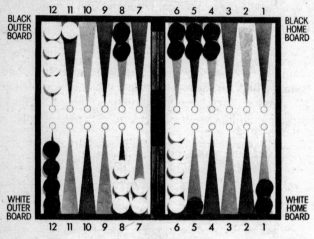

Diagram 63

White, at this stage, would like to make his 5 point, hitting the blot and removing that thorn from his side. If unable to do this—or to do it conveniently—he has to evaluate various factors.

Let's look at some of the alternatives:

(a) White throws 2–1. He could make the 5 point with this roll, but only at the expense of the bar point, where he would leave a blot. The safest way to maintain the advantage is to move unexcitingly from B 11 to B 12 and from W 8 to W 6.

(b) White throws 6–3. He could move his blot from B 11 and hit the man on W 5. That would be good play in many positions, but here it is unnecessarily dangerous. The blot on W 5 could be hit in 21 ways. Alternative plays are: the 6 from B 11 to W 8 and the 3 from the midpoint to W 10; or the 6 from the midpoint to W 7 and the 3 from B 11 to W 11. This second move, leaving a spare man on both W 8 and W 7, gives the pieces more scope. (To play the 6 to W 8 and the 3 to W 3 would be relatively safe for the moment, but White would need to cover the blot on W 3 very quickly.)

(c) White throws 6–4. He must leave a blot somewhere, and the choice is between running from B 11 to W 4 and playing the 4 to W 10 and the 6 to W 7. Which position appeals to you? The long move to W 4 is fractionally safer, as the blot there would be exposed to 14 shots, whereas a blot on W 10 would be exposed to 15 shots. But the move to W 10 and W 7 leaves White with a builder and two spare men in his outer board, splendidly poised for the kill. Again, 'better diversification'.

(d) White rolls 5–3 or 4–2. He could make a completely safe move with either of these throws, but he should not pass up the opportunity to make a fairly good point in his home board. The blot left on B 11 is open to 15 shots; even if it is hit, White will still have an equal game.

(e) White rolls 3–2, 4–3 or 5–4. With any of these rolls White will be happy to make a further point in his outer board, extending the block already formed and providing another safe point of entry for the men on B 12. For a development of that last notion, see 'Stepping-stones' in the next chapter.

All these moves, we venture to say, contain instructive points and are worth careful study. The three elements we mentioned—racing, containment and control—were all present. White, after his 6–6, was ahead and happy to avoid complications, but some of his moves were directed towards containment rather than safety. It is often right to accept a slight risk in order to establish a commanding position; we return to that theme in the chapter on the doubling cube.

Black did his best in the circumstances. Although White's back men had flown, he continued to make points on his board, hoping for a hit later on. And while holding a point on W 1 he posted a man on W 5 to give him some control of White's board.

So long as you threaten to contain your opponent, you can hold your game together even when you are far behind in the race.

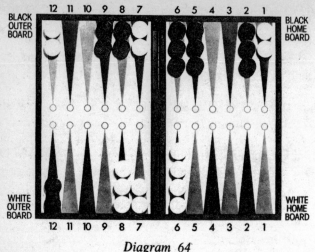

Diagram 64

Black is well ahead but White has strong defensive posts on B 1 and B 7.

White rolls 3–3. What should he play? He could bring his back men safely to B 7, normally a very good move, but that would betoken a complete misunderstanding of his tactical situation. The points on B 7 and B 1 are the strength of his game. He should leave the back points intact and hasten to make the 5 and 3 points. He can expect to hit sooner or later and must build up a good home board in preparation.

White rolls 5–4. He should not, as in Diagram 62, run from B 7, because he is not engaged in a running game. To move two men from W 8, slotting on W 4 and W 3, would show more understanding of the tactics required; but better still is to run a man from the midpoint to W 4. This attractive and expert play leaves White well placed to extend his 3-point block; he won't mind being hit on B 12, as to have another man back will give him more control over Black's home board; and so long as the blot remains, Black will have to be wary of moving just one man from the point opposite.

Study the next diagram carefully and ask yourself the question we posed at the beginning: as White, what are you trying to do?

86

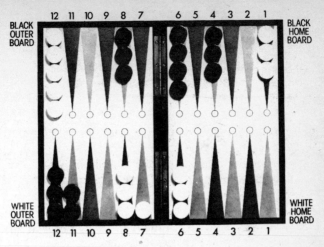

Diagram 65

As in the last diagram, Black is ahead, but White has a solid base at B1 and can develop his home board at leisure, hoping for the chance of a hit. The question is, can White do anything more positive?

White rolls 6–3. The obvious move is to make the White bar point and bring a builder to W10. That will leave a rather dead position in which you will be at a disadvantage. Black, being well ahead, will bring his men cautiously into his outer board, giving you at best a long shot from B1. Once round the corner, he won't find it difficult to bring his men safely into his home board. You, meanwhile, will be building up your home board in preparation for a hit that may never come. Experience of many similar games suggests that White will win about once in four. Black must leave a blot, White must hit it, and then White will still need to force the win.

How did you answer the question, 'What are you trying to do?' The answer should have been, 'Complicate the situation; if possible, find a move that will provide some counter-play'. The way to do that is to play the 3 to W10, as before, but the 6 from B1 to the bar point. As we noted when discussing opening moves, this blot is easily hit, but there are many good return shots. Suppose Black makes the fair roll of 4–2. He is more or less obliged to hit, because the man on B7 threatens his outer board and also may be covered by a 6 from B1. Coming from the bar, you can hit back with 13 shots; in addition, 5–4 will enable you to make Black's 5 point, 3–2 his 3 point. Quite

87

a wild game may develop, which in the present situation is all you can ask for.

The play to B 7 was a typical control move. We don't mean by this a move that puts White in control of the board: just one that increases command of space and contains a threat. The man on B 7 is like a sniper posted in the last house of a beleaguered street: not difficult to eliminate, but a nuisance while he's there.

The move would be unsound if it were not backed up by the point on B 1. When making this type of move you need a safe landing-place in Black's home board in case he is able to point on your blot. Otherwise you will be hit several times and will never get any sort of game going.

Moves that extend the range of the pieces may occur at any stage of the game. Here is an instructive end-game study:

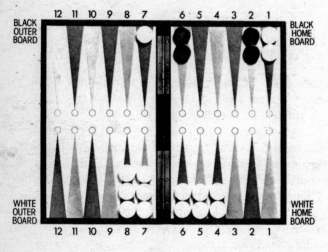

Diagram 66

Black has borne off eleven men but is likely to leave a blot before he can bear off the remainder. White's task is to give himself the maximum chance of a hit.

White rolls 3–2. He could play the full move from B 7, retaining the point on B 1. There are a few cases where it would turn out better for him to retain the point, but many more where the range of his pieces would be extended by splitting the back men. He plays the 2 to B 3, therefore, and the 3 from B 7 to B 10. Now 4–1 and 5–1 by Black both leave 23 shots.

Now make a small change in Black's home board, removing the men on B 6 and adding one to B 2. The position will be:

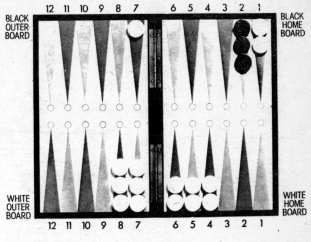

Diagram 67

It looks as though White is about to be gammoned, but Black's three men on his only point represent a hazard.

White rolls 5–3. Hoping that Black will throw a 1 and leave not one but two blots, White extends the range of his pieces by playing the 3 to B 4 and the 5 to W 3. He plays the 5 in this way to give himself the best chance of forming a prime. The game continues:

Black rolls 6–1. He bears off one man and is forced to hit with another, leaving two blots.

White rolls 4–1. He needed a little luck still, and here it is. He hits on B 1 and covers the blot on W 3, establishing his prime. The game is now evenly poised:

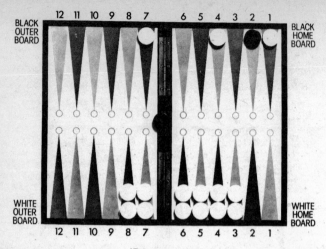

BLACK OUTER BOARD 12 11 10 9 8 7 6 5 4 3 2 1 **BLACK HOME BOARD**

WHITE OUTER BOARD 12 11 10 9 8 7 6 5 4 3 2 1 **WHITE HOME BOARD**

Diagram 68

As White has a prime from W 3 to W 8, the Black man
on the bar is completely hemmed in. White will aim
to put the other Black man on the bar as well.

White's tactics from now on will be to stay back with the man on B 1,
hoping for a hit. He has a good chance of this, because Black may
have to use his first 1 to come in from the bar. Even if Black is the
first to hit, White will have the chance of a return shot from the bar.

White needs to get two men back because he will have to vacate
the high points sooner or later and Black, with only one man to bring
round and two to bear off, will be about 10 to 1 on to win the race.
But if White can force two men back he will have an excellent chance
to bear off several men before both have made their escape. In fact,
White would be favourite; a triumph for containment and control!

CHAPTER EIGHT

Tactical Strokes in the Middle Game

There are various tactical themes in backgammon which occur quite often and are easy to understand once you have the general idea in mind. We discuss in this chapter:

1. Slotting.
2. Stepping-stones.
3. Duplicators.
4. Double jeopardy.
5. Options.

1 Slotting

We have given many examples of slotting in the early chapters without, perhaps, commenting directly on the advantages to be gained from this type of play. When you slot on a critical point you greatly increase your chances of making that point with a subsequent throw. Take the opening throw of 5–1, for example, where the standard play for White is to move a man from the midpoint to W 8 and to drop a man down from the 6 point, slotting on 5. If this blot on 5 is not hit you can cover it with any 3 or 1 (20 shots), plus 4–4, 2–2 and 6–2, a total of 24 shots. Compare that with your chance of making the 5 point on your second turn if you have not slotted and have not brought a builder into the outer board: you can do it only with 3–1, 1–1, 3–3 and 4–4, just 5 shots.

Moves based on this principle occur throughout the play:

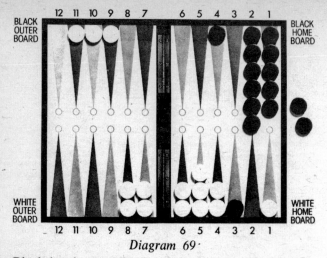

Diagram 69

Black has borne off two men but a blot has been hit and now he has a back man facing a 5-point prime. White's aim is to prevent this piece from escaping.

White throws 6–4. He could bring in any of the men from Black's outer board and still be a good favourite, but there is a stronger move than this: play the 6 to W 9 and the 4 to W 12, leaving this position:

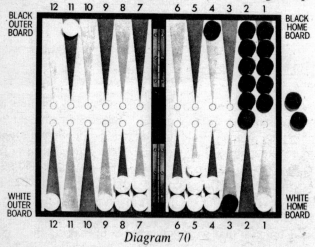

Diagram 70

Black can still escape with a 6 and in doing so will hit at least one blot, possibly two. But sending these men to the bar will simply strengthen White's defence at the back.

92

If Black fails to throw a 6 on his next turn White will be able to cover the blot on W 9 with 25 shots. Throws of 6–2 and 2–2 will enable him to point on W 3, completing a prime at that end. With 6–4 or 6–1, also, White will hit the blot, not fearing a return shot.

Here is another situation where a move that looks risky in fact represents White's best chance to wrap up the game:

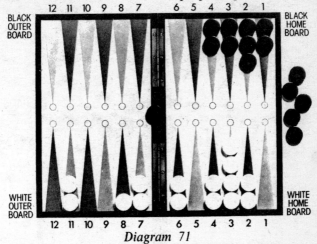

Diagram 71

Black has borne off five men and will win the game if his man on the bar can enter and escape before White has begun to bear off.

White rolls 6–1. The (temporarily) safe move is to play the 6 from W 8 and the 1 from W 3. Black will then have the advantage if he throws 5–3, 5–4 or 5–5. The weakness of this move by White is that if Black fails to throw a 5 and stays on the bar, his prospects will improve when White is obliged to bring in men from his outer board. It is therefore sensible for White to force the issue by slotting on W 5 with the 6 from W 11 and playing the 1 from W 11 to W 10. Black may escape now by throwing 5–3 or better, but he is unlikely to have a second chance; if he fails to come in at once, he will probably lose the game.

Why does White, having moved from W 11 to W 5, play the 1 from W 11 to W 10 rather than from W 3 to W 2? Because if Black manages to roll 6–5 White will have only one man on the bar and will have a better chance to stop the last Black man on the way round. If Black is going to roll 5–5 it won't make any difference whether White has one or two men on the bar.

93

2 Stepping-stones

It is good tactics, whenever possible, to keep one's pieces within easy communication of one another. One of the advantages of establishing a point in the opponent's home board is that you then have a safe landing-place from the bar, and one of the advantages of establishing points in your own home board is that you can bring men safely and smoothly to these points.

It is desirable to maintain the same sort of links in the middle of the board. You may recall this situation from the last chapter (Diagram 63):

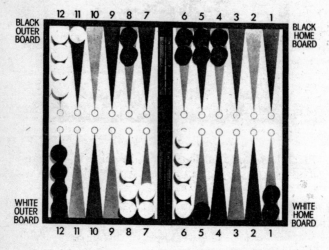

Diagram 72

One of White's problems is to bring in his outside men without leaving a blot on the midpoint or in his outer board.

We remarked that White, if unable to point effectively on W 5, would be happy to establish another point in his outer board with 3–2, 4–3 or 5–4. Any of these points would assist him to move away from his midpoint without leaving a blot in his outer board. The extra point would act as a bridge, resting-place, stepping-stone—call it what you will.

Of course, you will often be left with a back man—perhaps a casualty from a late hit—and no help within close range. That is the situation in the following game:

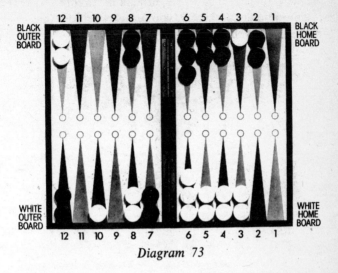

Diagram 73

White's back man is weak and Black has the better game for that reason.

White throws 5–3. He cannot move the man on B 3, but he can cover the blot on W 10 and move the other man on the midpoint to safety at W 8. It looks quite neat, but the play would be wrong for two reasons: first, it would leave the back man weaker still; second, the departure from the midpoint would be a relief to Black's men on W 7. At the moment, the best feature in White's game is that Black may have difficulty in bringing these men round without leaving a blot.

The best play with 5–3 is to run a man from W 10 to W 2. White won't be out of danger, but so long as he holds the midpoint his game need not be lost.

3 Duplicators

A 'duplicator' is a move that reduces the opponent's chances by offering him fewer targets. For example, instead of leaving two blots that can be hit by different numbers, you leave two blots that can both be hit by the same number.

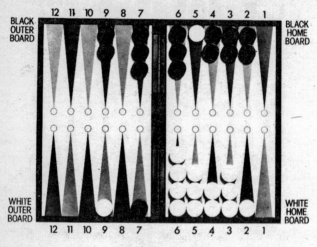

Diagram 74

White is far ahead but his back man still has four hurdles to surmount. Even if he can get round the first three, there is still the man on W 7 to reckon with.

White throws 3–1. He could bring in the man on W 9, but in that case he would hear from the solicitors of the blot left defenceless on B 5. He might play from B 5 to B 8 and cover the blot on W 2. Not good either, for now he would be exposed to any 1 or 2, and Black has quite a formidable home board. Having played the 3 to B 8, White should play the 1 from W 9 to W 8; then Black can hit only with a 1 in either place (or with a long-ranger from W 7). And suppose Black misses, with an average roll such as 3–2: then the hunter (on W 7) will become the hunted.

In Chapter 4 (Diagram 40) we met an example of a duplicator on the second move of the game:

96

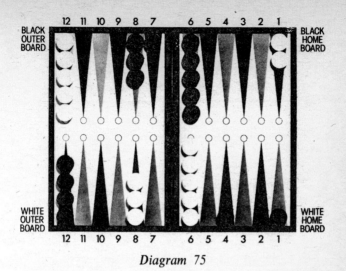

Diagram 75

Black has opened with 6–3. He has played one man to his bar point and has split his back men. White now rolls 5–3.

The normal move with 5–3 is to play from the midpoint to W 8 and to bring a builder to W 10. That looks dangerous here because the blot on W 10 would be exposed to a direct 6. On second thoughts, however, White realizes that if Black throws a 6 he will be as keen to make his bar point as to hit the blot; thus the play to W 10 is a duplicator, presenting Black (should he throw a 6) with what bridge players call 'duplication of values'.

There is another possibility in the diagram position. White could hit on W 1 and play the 3 from B 1 to B 4. Then a 1 would be a duplicator for Black, in the sense that he would be torn between hitting on W 1 and making his bar point.

Reverse duplicators

The object of a duplicator is to restrict the opponent so that fewer good moves will be available for him. A player wants to do the opposite for himself: he aims to extend the choices that will be open to him on his next turn. The principle of a 'reverse duplicator' is seen in this example:

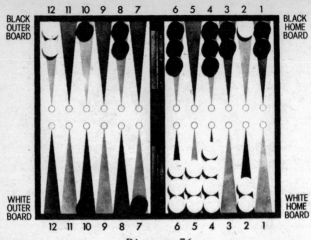

Diagram 76

White's back man is in some jeopardy, but Black has two men unprotected in White's outer board. White will have the initiative if he can hit one of these.

White throws 3–1. He could move his back man a small distance but it is better to keep Black busy by hitting the blot on W 10. But what about the 1? Observing that an advance to W 9 would expose him to 6–3 from the bar, White might think of playing the 1 from the midpoint. What's wrong with that? Well, look at the new position:

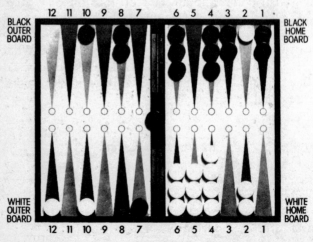

Diagram 77

98

If Black failed to enter on his next turn, White would
wish either to escape with his back man or to put
another man on the bar.

Suppose that Black throws 6–4 and stays on the bar. Now a 5 or 3
would be good for White on either side of the board, but combinations
such as 6–2 or 6–4 or 6–1 or 4–2 would be of little use to him. He
has, as it were, prepared a duplicator for himself.

Now restore the man on W 12 to B 12 and play the 1 (in Diagram
76) from W 10 to W 9. Suddenly, good moves are available with any
2, 3, 5 or 6. As for the danger of Black coming in from the bar with
6–3, you may observe that a 6 is a duplicator for him, whether he comes
in at W 1 or W 3.

4 Double jeopardy

There is a kinship between duplicators and 'double jeopardy'. The
principle of double jeopardy is that when your opponent needs a particular lucky shot you must take care not to present him with a bonus.

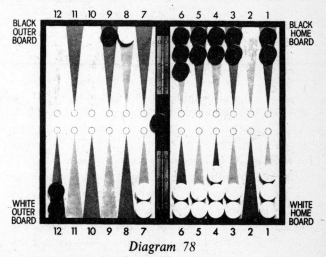

Diagram 78

White is well ahead and his only worry, it seems, is
to bring round the man on B 8.

White rolls 6–3. Glad to have surmounted the remaining obstacles,
he comes bounding along to W 11 and thence to W 8. Then Black
throws the magical 6–2, not only coming off the bar but hitting the
blot White has foolishly left. As 6–2 was the only throw that would

enable the man on the bar to enter and escape from the block, White should have been on guard against it. All he had to do was play the 3 from W 4 to W 1.

In this next example it is easier to overlook the danger:

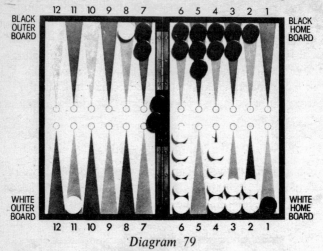

Diagram 79

There is no weakness in White's game. Black is in desperate trouble, with two men on the bar and one languishing on W 1.

White rolls 5–2. With his thoughts on a gammon, White brings the man on W 11 to W 6 and advances the man on B 8 to B 10. Then disaster strikes. Black throws 5–5, and after entering both men at W 5 he has enough steam left to hit the blot on B 10. If White doesn't come in at once with a 2 he will probably lose the game.

As 5–5 was the only throw to be feared, White should have been careful not to stop anywhere on the same railway line. Thus to go from B 8 to W 10 would have been an equal error.

Can you see White's best move in the diagram position? He should play the 5 from B 8 to W 12 and the 2 from W 4 to W 2, increasing his chance to point on the blot on W 1.

5 Options

You don't need to play backgammon for long before you meet situations where a particular number, usually a 5 or a 6, is most awkward to play; and you realize that if you had played your previous turn differently you would have avoided the present impasse.

One of the skills in the game is to preserve options so that you don't fall into this trap. First, you need to see in time what number will be awkward; then you have to organize so that you will have an alternative should the awkward number turn up.

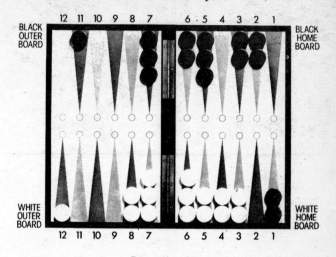

Diagram 80

White's game is obviously very strong. He may be forced to leave a blot eventually while bearing off, but for the present he appears to be safe.

White rolls 4–2.   He sees no reason not to bring in the man from W 12 to W 6. His mistake becomes apparent when on the next turn he throws 6–1, 6–2 or 6–3 and is obliged to break the prime and to leave a blot in his home board.

Here White has failed to observe that if he brings in the man from W 12, 6s will be an awkward number for him. Best, in the diagram position, is to play from W 12 to W 8 and from W 6 to W 4. Now a 6 can be played without breaking the prime. To leave a blot in front of a prime is of course no disadvantage.

It is especially important to preserve options when otherwise a long throw would compel you to break up a treasured point in the opponent's home board.

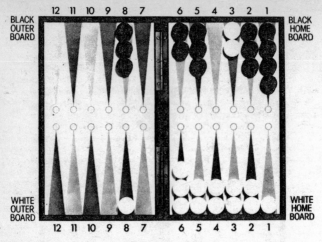

Diagram 81

White's only hope to save the game is to throw 6–6
or score a late hit with his back men.

White rolls 4–3. He does not want to disturb his point on B 3,
obviously. It seems natural play to move the man on W 8 to W 1, completing a prime. But that might well turn out to be an error. Black's
board is not too well organized and there is a good chance that he will
present you with at least an opportunity for a hit. The last thing you
want to do is throw a 6 and be forced to break up your point on B 3.
You may have to run from there later to avoid being gammoned, but
your chances of saving the game rest on maintaining the point while
there is any chance of scoring a hit.

The way to play 4–3 in the diagram position is to make both moves
from your 5 point. You will preserve a 5-point board for as long as
you can and your chance for a hit, if it is going to come at all, will
come soon.

CHAPTER NINE

Pacing and the Back Game

One of the unique features of backgammon is that if you are far behind in the race you can go into reverse and, if you are lucky, force a re-run. It is as though a runner in a track race who was in danger of being lapped could turn round, hamper his opponent, and later join him in the run-in on equal terms.

This is the famous 'back game'. It is a difficult subject and it may be helpful to set out in advance the train of thought we intend to follow in this chapter:

1. *A defensive or semi-back game, as opposed to a true back game* (Diagram 82).
2. *A back game that has gone wrong* (Diagram 83).
3. *What a successful back game should look like* (Diagrams 84 to 86).
4. *How to move into a back game* (Diagrams 87 to 90).
5. *Don't hit until you are ready* (Diagram 91).
6. *The best points to hold for a back game* (Diagrams 92 and 93).

1 A defensive or semi-back game, as opposed to a true back game

You may recall this position which arose from Diagram 59 in Chapter 6:

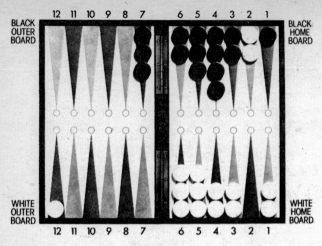

Diagram 82

White's last throw, previous to this diagram, was 6–6. He could have run his two back men to W 11, but as he would have had no chance in a running game he played instead two men from the midpoint to W 1. As the board stands now, he may well get the chance of a hit and meanwhile, with one man still on W 12 and spare men on W 6 and W 5, he has room to move without breaking up his board.

This is a typical defensive position, but not a true back game. White's back men have been hemmed in, making it dangerous for him to run with one of them. He has stayed back, maintaining his point and hoping to get a shot. His position is far from promising but he has some chance because of the factor we mentioned—that he has room to move in his own board. Had the man on W 12 been situated on W 1, for example, he would very quickly have been forced to break up points in his own board; once that has happened, a hit will be less effective because Black will easily come off the bar.

2 A back game that has gone wrong

The majority of back games break down for this reason: White gets too far ahead, so that, when he does succeed in hitting, his defensive wall has crumbled. He arrives in this sort of position:

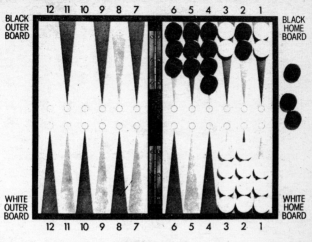

Diagram 83

White has two points in his opponent's home board—essential elements in a back game—and is likely to get a hit if he can maintain them. His prospects are nevertheless very poor.

There are two grave disadvantages in White's position: if he throws any 4, 5 or 6 he must abandon one of the defensive points in Black's board; and if he does hit a blot he has no chance to contain his opponent. This is called a 'nothing game', because White has nothing to play for. Incidentally, the Black pieces in this diagram, considering the circumstances, are particularly well organized. Although White holds two good points, 5–3 is the only throw that will force Black to leave a blot on his next turn.

3 What a successful back game should look like

This is what a back game *should* look like:

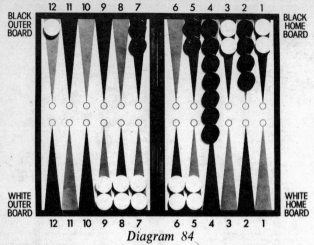

Diagram 84

> White has two good points in his opponent's home board and good chances of containment if he does score a hit.

Why is this such a promising situation for White? It is worth noting the favourable elements in his position:

He holds the best points in Black's board—1 and 3.

Though he disposes of only ten men in his front board he has constructed a 5-point prime.

This prime is situated in the best area. A Black man on the bar could make a rapid escape only by throwing 6–4. Also, White has room to move forward without spoiling his position; a 5-point prime between 4 and 8 or 3 and 7 would contain the opponent equally well. White is ready to hit, but not in a hurry to do so.

It is to White's advantage that a Black man on the bar should have space in which to enter. If such a man enters but does not escape, Black will be forced to make moves on his own side of the board, so that shortly he will have nothing but long columns on his two lowest points.

White's man on B 12, being some way back, allows him to make a move or two without compromising his position elsewhere.

Now consider Black's position. As a result of desperate attempts not to leave a blot, he has given up his 6 point and has only a 3-point board. As soon as the men on B 7 have been brought in, all the White pieces will be able to move out with impunity.

Let's carry on with this game for a few rolls and see how things develop.

Black throws 6–3. This is one of 16 rolls that compel him to leave a blot, but at least he has a choice. He cannot play the 6. He can play the 3 from his 5 point, leaving 20 return shots, or from the bar point, leaving 24 return shots. Despite the greater immediate risk, it is better play to move from the bar point for two reasons: he retains a 3-point board, which may conceivably help him later on; and if he does escape being hit he will have only one man to bring in and may succeed in bearing off without further accident.

White rolls 5–2. Unlucky, he misses the blot. He moves from the mid-point to his 6 point, keeping his block intact.

Black rolls 6–4. He cannot move.

White throws 6–1. He hits the blot and continues with the same piece to B 8.

Black throws 4–3. He is happy to come in on 4 because from there he could surmount the wall with a 6. The 3 is not so good; he will prefer to hit on B 1, obviously, rather than leave a blot on B 5. The position is now:

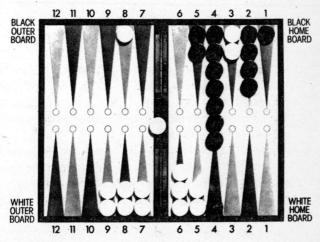

Diagram 85

White should be able to come off the bar quite easily and move his men round, while keeping the opponent's back man under control.

White rolls 2–1. Nothing wrong with that; he enters on B 1, hitting the blot, and hits on W 4 as well. He is glad of the chance to remove this man from a point where it could escape with a direct shot.

Black rolls 6–3. He enters on 3 and still has a man on the bar.

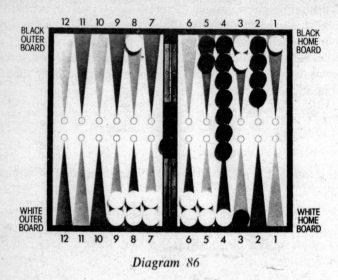

Diagram 86

White's game is going according to plan. He has forced two men back and his 5-point prime is still intact.

White is almost sure to win now, so long as he follows the right tactics. His main objective is to form a 6-point prime; meanwhile, so long as he does not spoil the semi-prime he holds at the moment, he will keep Black busy by hitting repeatedly and putting two men on the bar.

Thus, with *any* 1 White will hit on W 3. With 6–1 he will hit and make the 3 point. With 6–5 he will hit and make the 4 point; with 5–4 the same, though for the moment he will be reducing his block from five points to four. When unable both to hit and retain at least a 4-point block, White will move round the man on B 8, and after that the man on B 1. Black will need miracle throws to escape with both back men, and even then White will still have a rearguard to pick them up as they come round. When White has completed his prime he will edge it along to the right, stifling his opponent and playing for a gammon.

4 How to move into a back game

We come now to the heart of the matter, which is how to pace yourself so that when you enter into a back game your timing will be right. A well-timed back game, such as that beginning with Diagram 84, will win more often than not, but it must be said that one does not set out to play such a game deliberately. Too often, one or two high doubles will ruin the position at the critical moment, forcing the player to break up his wall; and if you lose such a game it will often be a gammon.

On the other hand, whenever your opponent has started well by making points and hitting a few blots, you must consider going into reverse and preparing for a back game.

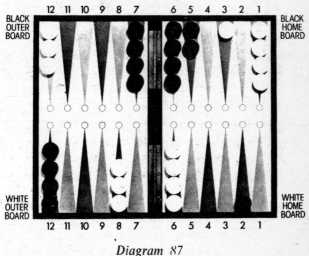

Diagram 87

White has been sent to the bar three times and has made no extra points. Black still has one man back, but White has little chance of containing it.

White's game is in poor shape. If he were so doom-conscious as to count the pips he would find that Black's count was 137 and his own 205—far more than at the start of the game.

As White has very little chance of making up the deficit, his thoughts must turn to a back game. His first objective is to make a second point in Black's home board; the 3 point would be best, but any other would be acceptable. After that, he must get his timing right. By the time that Black has brought all his men round and is likely to leave a blot, White wants to be able to contain, or at least intercept, any man that is sent to the bar.

Almost always, the problem in pacing is not to get too far ahead. If you are lying well back when you begin to hit you will still be in the game with good chances; but if you are too far forward—in a 'nothing' game—the Black men will sail round the board without opposition.

Although, as we have observed, White is a long way behind, he is not yet far enough behind. How does one judge that? Well, consider how far each player has to travel before the critical stage is reached. When that moment arrives, Black will have all his men in, or close to, his home board; White will have four men back and with his remaining men he will have aimed to form a 5-point block, either in his home board or just outside it. Black, at the moment, has nine men outside his home board; White has at most seven to bring round because, remember, he will be leaving four at the back. Thus, as we said at the beginning, White is still too far ahead.

How, then, is White to slow himself down? Unless he is lucky enough to roll much lower dice than his opponent he can go backwards only by leaving blots and forcing Black to hit them. Now that the tactical objective is understood, let's proceed with the game.

White rolls 6–2. With the 2 he makes the Black 3 point. What about the 6? Breaking all the normal rules of strategy, he hits the blot on W 2. His general plan is to leave blots in his home board and force Black to hit them.

Black rolls 4–2. Knowing what his opponent is trying to do, he avoids hitting on W 2. He comes in at W 4 and plays the 2 from his midpoint.

White rolls 2–1. That fits in with his plan very well. He hits on W 4 with the 2. And the 1? Quite right, he slots on W 5. The board now looks like this:

110

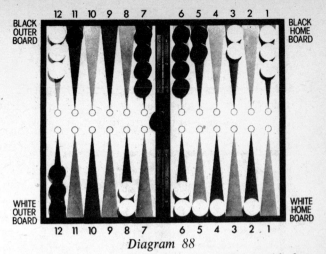

Diagram 88

White has six men to bring into his home board before his back game begins, while Black has nine. Thus White is still too far ahead. He hopes Black will be forced to hit one of the blots.

Black rolls 6–3. Maddening, he escapes to W 9 without hitting.

White rolls 4–3. Better! He hits on W 9 with the 4 and slots on W 3, leaving this comic opera position:

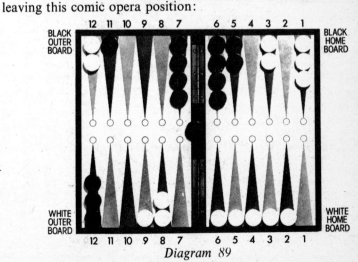

Diagram 89

White still has six men to bring round, and Black nine, but this time Black will scarcely be able to avoid hitting one of the blots.

111

Black rolls 3–3. He hits on W 3, perforce, makes his own 4 point, and plays the fourth move from his midpoint.

White rolls 6–3. He comes in on B 3 and hits with the 6 on W 3, leaving five blots again.

Black rolls 5–4. He comes in at W 5, choosing to disrupt the 5 point rather than the 4 point, and continues with the same piece to W 9. We will leave the game now in this intriguing position:

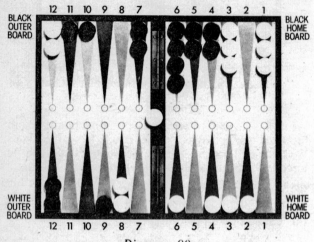

Diagram 90

Now White has seven free men to bring round to his home board, and so has Black. As White has a man on the bar and two (apart from the intended back men) in his opponent's home board, he is now far enough back.

It has been hard work, but White's pacing is now about right. His next objective is to bring the three spare men into play (from the bar and from B 1 and B 3). He won't mind leaving blots as he moves these men out because, as we said earlier, it is better to be too far behind than too far ahead.

So White will attempt to bring his spare men out and to form a block, probably from W 3 to W 7. No matter if the man on W 2 is hit; White may be glad to bring it round the board again. Black, meanwhile, will step delicately and leave as few blots as possible when bearing off. White may be gammoned if he doesn't hit at the right time, but whatever happens it will have been an exciting game.

112

5 Don't hit until you are ready

Many back games are wrecked because of a premature sortie from the defensive position. Study this situation:

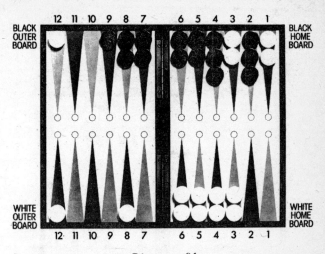

Diagram 91

White's timing for a back game is quite good. He holds two points in his opponent's board and has fair chances of containment.

White rolls 6–3. It is tempting to swoop on the blot at B 9, but consider the effect of doing this. Black will not find it too difficult to enter from the bar—and it won't kill him if he stays on the bar for a couple of turns. White will need several good throws to bring out his back men, and soon he will be falling over his feet in his home board.

In the diagram position White must hold his fire. If not sent to the bar, Black will soon be forced to break up his higher points. White will almost surely have chances for a hit before long, and when he does hit the way will be clear for his back men to escape.

What, then, is the best way to play 6–3? White might think of slotting on W 2 and playing the 3 from B 12. There is a better move than that: play the 6 from the midpoint to the bar point and the 3 from W 12 to W 9. Then any 1 or 2 will make the bar point, and if neither of these numbers turns up White may slot on the 2 point.

6 The best points to hold in a back game

In all the examples of a back game we have credited White with the 1 and 3 points in his opponent's home board. Those are the best points to hold. Other good combinations are 1 and 2, 1 and 4, 2 and 3, 2 and 4.

You may wonder why 1–3 is preferable to 1–2, since the opponent can, and invariably will, by-pass the 3 and establish a point on 2. A couple of examples will quickly make the point clear.

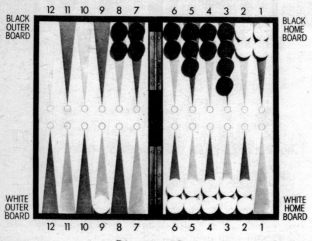

Diagram 92

It is Black's turn to roll and the position is very tight. White needs to hit quickly, because otherwise he will have to break up his home board.

In this type of end-game both players would be happy not to have to move at all. Usually a 6 is the worst number to throw at such a time, but here Black cannot play a 6. It is true that with 6–5, 6–4 or 6–3 he will have to leave a blot, but in each case he will make the single move from B 8 and White will be able to hit only with a direct 6; and even then the other back men will not be free. Note, also, that if Black throws 6–6 he does not need to move at all, and he plays only half the move with 5–5.

Other contiguous points have the same drawback—that the opponent will be unable to play one or other of the high numbers. Suppose, for example, that White holds the 2 and 3 points and that Black has the same points in his outer board as in the diagram above.

He will be unable to play any 5, and with a 6 he will sneak behind the White defences.

Now contrast the situation with 1 and 3:

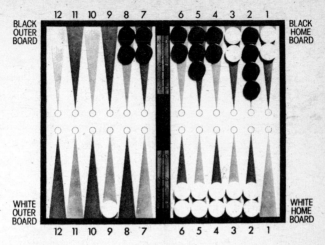

Diagram 93

The board is the same as in the last diagram, except that White now holds the 1 and 3 points and the Black men on B 3 have been moved to B 2.

Black can now play any 5 or 6, speeding along to his disadvantage. No roll leaves a single blot *for the moment*, but 6–5 and 5–4 each leave a pitiful double blot. Black can play half the roll with 6–6 or 5–5, and 4–4 leaves horrible gaps. However the play develops after that roll, there will be no danger of the back men being shut in.

Of course, a player cannot always choose which points he will hold in his opponent's board. Nevertheless, in a long game where several blots are hit, there are usually opportunities to establish one point rather than another. In any case, it is essential to know, whether you are on the attack or the defence, that 1–3 is a formidable combination, while some other holdings are not so effective for the purpose of a back game.

CHAPTER TEN

The Doubling Cube

The doubling cube gives backgammon its salt and savour, making it the perfect medium for everyone who enjoys a battle of wits and a sporting enterprise. The cube is also a most important element in success. Most players learn to move the pieces reasonably well and inferior moves do not, as in chess at a high level, necessarily cost the game; they may even turn out better than the mathematically superior play. But follies with the cube are seldom forgiven and are expensive. As golfers say of a comparable situation, you drive for fun but you putt for money.

We must begin with a warning that this will not be an easy chapter. We tackle some difficult problems head on, because they are vital to success. These are the main subjects:

1. *How the cube is used and exchanged.*
2. *The odds required for doubling, accepting, redoubling, and beavering* (Diagram 94).
3. *How to judge whether you are worth a double in the early or middle game* (Diagrams 95 and 96).
4. *How to judge whether to accept a double in the early or middle game* (Diagram 97).
5. *Why it is usually right to double when you have the advantage* (Diagram 98).
6. *When you are too good to double* (Diagram 99).
7. *Doubling in the end game* (Diagram 100).

1 How the cube is used and exchanged

As explained in the opening chapter, the cube is originally set at a high number to indicate that it has not so far come into operation. In effect, it stands at 1, but there is no 1 on the cube. If the opening throw is a double the cube may, by prior agreement, be turned to 2— an 'automatic double'. At any time in the game a player whose turn it is to throw may turn the cube to the next number, offering to double the stake. He passes it to his opponent, who may drop, conceding the game at the present level, or accept. If he accepts, the stake is increased to the new figure, the cube remains on his side, and only he can offer the next double. There is no limit to the number of doubles that can be made in a single game.

There is an optional variation, known as a 'beaver', whereby a player who has been doubled may *immediately* redouble. As a reward for his confidence, he keeps possession of the cube.

2 The odds required for doubling, accepting, redoubling, and beavering

On the surface, it may seem that a player who has a better than even chance of winning the game should always be happy to increase the stakes. This may be the case at the very end of the game, when there is no more room for tactical manoeuvre, but until that stage a player who thinks of doubling must take into account that he is giving his opponent possession of the cube. Here is a brief example to show the tactical disadvantage incurred by a player who has doubled or redoubled:

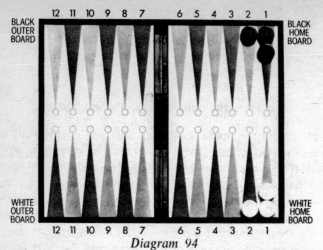

BLACK OUTER BOARD

BLACK HOME BOARD

WHITE OUTER BOARD

WHITE HOME BOARD

12 11 10 9 8 7   6 5 4 3 2 1

Diagram 94

The player who has the throw is obviously a strong favourite at this stage, but the position of the cube is important, too.

It is White's turn. If there were no cube you would work out his chances in the following way:

As 6 of the possible 36 throws are doubles, it is 30 to 6, i.e. 5 to 1, against throwing a double. White throws first and there are 5 chances in 6 that he will *not* throw a double. There is then 1 chance in 6 that Black will throw a double on the final turn. Multiply these fractions $\left(\frac{5}{6} \times \frac{1}{6}\right)$ and the answer, 5 over 36, represents Black's chance to win the game. He is 31 to 5, just over 6 to 1, against.

If you are not used to calculating in that sort of way, there is another method. To avoid fractions, assume a series of 36 games in which the present situation arises. White will begin with a double 6 times, finishing the game. On the other 30 occasions Black will have the final roll and will throw a double 5 times (once in 6). So Black will win the game 5 times in 36, the same figure as before.

These odds represent the chances if Black has the cube, so that White cannot double. But if the cube is in the centre or on White's side, White will double and his opponent, being 6 to 1 against, will obviously not be able to accept. Thus White will escape the possible aggravation of losing to a double on the final throw.

If you look at the same example from Black's angle you will see another aspect of the same proposition. Suppose that Black has at one time held the cube but has surrendered it by redoubling. When this end situation arises, Black will regret his former action not only because the stake is higher but also because he will have to abandon the game when White doubles. If Black still held the cube he would be able to play out the game to the finish.

To compensate for the handicap of passing the cube to his opponent, a player who contemplates a double at any time before the last two throws requires odds of at least 11 to 8 in his favour.

We are speaking there of the *first* double in the game. *A player who makes the second or any subsequent double requires still better odds in his favour—about 7 to 4.*

Very few players are aware of this distinction, let alone the reason for it. The reason is that there is a difference between letting the opponent take control of a cube which was in the centre and letting him take control of a cube which you held yourself. So long as the cube is on your side you are safe from a redouble, should the game take an unpleasant turn. So we repeat: there is a difference between the first double, which moves the cube from the centre to your opponent, and a redouble, which moves the cube from your corner to his.

Now let's consider the situation of the player who is doubled. The break-even point for him, in strict mathematics, is 3 to 1 against. That is to say, *if he estimates that he has one chance in four of winning the game, he is right to accept.* In case you find that figure surprising, apply this little test:

Half way through the game your opponent doubles. Suppose that on each of four occasions when this happens you decide to drop. Your net loss on the four games is 4 points.

Suppose, next, that on each of the four occasions you accept. He wins three times, you win once. His three wins bring him in 6 points, your win is worth 2 points. Your net loss is again 4 points. Conclusion: by winning one game in four you achieve the same result as if you had retired on each occasion.

Two other factors enter into the calculation. You are entitled to take into account the fact that you are obtaining possession of the cube. That is an added reason for accepting. But there is often a stronger point on the other side—the danger that you may be gammoned. If you accept a double and are later gammoned you lose four times the original stake. As we shall see when we consider the practical side of all this, a player who is doubled must examine the gammon possibilities very closely. (By the same token, a shrewd player will double more lightly than usual when he knows that his opponent will be apprehensive of a gammon.)

If beavers are played, when is it right to beaver? At any time when the chances, as you see them, are about even or slightly against you. Here, again, you are entitled to take into account that the cube will be on your side.

However, there is a strong psychological element in beavering. If your opponent is quick to double it is good tactics to let him know that you are always prepared to beaver. But if, perhaps because he is losing or is a gambler, he makes obviously *bad* doubles, it is better just to accept them with a show of dubiety and let him continue in his foolish ways.

To sum up this section in general terms rather than in terms of figures, you need fair odds in your favour before making the first double of the game; somewhat better odds when you make any subsequent double, transferring the cube from your corner to that of your opponent. When you are doubled you may accept if you have a reasonable chance to win (one in four), but you must be cautious when there is a possibility that you may be gammoned. You are entitled to beaver whenever you think that your opponent's game is very little, if at all, better than your own.

One point we have not mentioned is the *level* of the doubles. To double from 1 to 2, risking a redouble to 4, is one thing; to double near the end from 8 to 16, knowing that if you don't throw well he will come back with 32 and you will have to accept though the odds will be unpleasantly against you, is another. Should this affect your action? Logically, no. If you have a sound double from 2 to 4, you have a sound double from 8 to 16. But in a finite and imperfect world there may be other considerations. Certainly, if you reckon to be the better player, you don't want to risk a very big turnover on a single throw.

3 How to judge whether you are worth a double in the early or middle game

Having established the odds required for different ventures, we turn to the more difficult question of judging whether the necessary odds exist. On this matter, it is impossible to avoid the discouraging remark that when a game can take so many forms, only experience will enable a player to judge how likely he is to win the contest.

However, there are a number of general tests that can be usefully applied. You may ask yourself how successful, as compared with your opponent, you have been in achieving the standard objectives of racing, containment, and control. You look for these favourable elements:

Have you constructed at least a 4-point block?

Have you made at least one extra point in your home board?

Have your back men escaped? If not, does your opponent threaten to contain them?

If it is likely that there will be no further contact, are you reasonably ahead in a running game?

What is 'reasonably ahead'? There is a formula that can be applied quite early or quite late in the game. You count the pips on the two sides (see Chapter 6) and note the difference, which presumably will be in your favour (since you are contemplating a double). *If your lead is as much as $\frac{1}{12}$ of your total, you have a fair double.* This formula takes into account that it is your turn to throw.

You may recall this situation from Chapter 6 (Diagram 57):

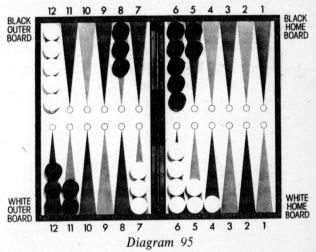

Diagram 95

White has the throw and a small lead in most sections of the board. The problem is, does his lead justify a double?

The count of pips, as we noted earlier, is 124 for White, 131 for Black. White's lead is 7—less than $\frac{1}{12}$ of his total. The conclusion is that a double would be premature. Now advance a man from B 12 to W 10. White would then have a lead of 10 and his total would be 121; just enough for a double.

This method of calculation can be applied until the total of pips descends below 50 or so. When you begin to bear off, the make-up of the home board becomes a critical factor, as we shall see later.

Sometimes your advantage will consist not so much in the virtues of your own position as in the weakness of your opponent's. Here Black's game is compromised in the first three rolls:

Black rolls 6–2 and slots on his 5 point.

White rolls 6–1 and makes his bar point.

Black rolls 6–5. Unable to move either back man, he plays from the midpoint to B 8 and B 7.

White rolls 3–2 and brings builders to W 11 and W 10.

Black rolls 5–5. This throw, maintaining its baleful reputation, forces him to play the last two men from his midpoint and make his 3 point. The board now looks like this:

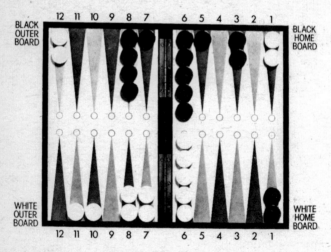

Diagram 96

Black not only has two blots exposed but has left his midfield completely open. He has no room for manoeuvre and no support for his back men.

Although White has made only two rolls, one of them very ordinary, he will double. If Black is sensible he will prefer to fight another day.

4 How to judge whether to accept a double in the early or middle game

As we have said, a player is entitled to accept a double when he has one chance in four of winning the game and is not in danger of being gammoned. When the opponent (Black) has simply made a better start to the game, making a 4-point block while White has thrown poorly and made no progress, it is reasonable to accept a double unless one's game contains a particular weakness. A 5-point prime in the opponent's board is always a formidable obstacle, especially if White's back man is not adjacent to the block and will need two specific throws, perhaps a 2 and a 6, to escape. When that is the situation, or when the opponent has a 6-point prime, there is obvious danger of a gammon.

Sometimes it is clear that the fate of the game will depend on specific chances which can be calculated with fair accuracy.

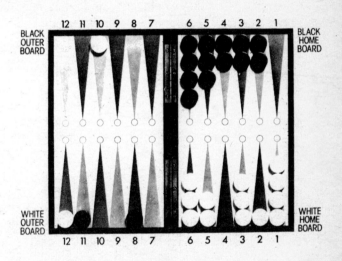

Diagram 97

It is Black's turn to roll, and he doubles. White is under fire from two men, and if hit he will face a formidable block.

White may think at first that he is almost certain to be put on the bar, but a closer look will reveal that Black's chances of hitting are not so good as they usually are when two men have two targets within fairly close range. The White piece on W 12 is exposed to any 4 or 1 (20 shots) plus 2–2. As 4s are duplicators, the only extra shot, against the man on B 10, is 5–2. Thus White is exposed to 23 shots out of 36. That makes him 7 to 4 against, and so far he has a fair take.

However, there are two more factors. If White is hit—and especially if two men are hit—he may be gammoned. Secondly, if White escapes being hit he will have the advantage but the game will not be over. These considerations tip the balance against accepting the double.

Finally, suppose you are doubled in what looks like being a running game. We have said that a player who is ahead has a double if his lead in pips amounts to $\frac{1}{12}$ of his total. *The formula for accepting a double is that the opponent's lead should not be more than $\frac{1}{7}$ of his total.*

Look once more at Diagram 95 and mentally transfer a White piece from B 12 to W 4. The lead will then be 16 and White's total 115. As 16 is just under $\frac{1}{7}$ of 115, this would be a borderline decision for Black.

5 Why it is usually right to double when you have the advantage

This may not strike you as a problem, but it is possible to get some wrong ideas. A player who has a fair lead in a running game may argue along these lines:

'I am ahead, at least 6 to 4 on to win, but why shouldn't I wait a turn or two before doubling? If I throw a low number and my opponent throws a high double, the position will be reversed and I shall be glad I didn't double. If the next two throws are about even, my lead will be confirmed and I will double then.'

The fallacy in this argument is that the player in the lead is as likely as his opponent to make the next good throw, and if he doubles after the good throw it will be too late. As at poker, the winning player keeps his opponent at full stretch, doubling all the time on small, but adequate, margins.

Another false argument is often raised when a player has the better prospects but is nervous about his next throw.

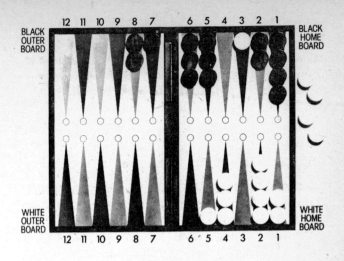

Diagram 98

White has borne off four men but has been hit and needs now to extricate the piece on B 3.

It is White's throw, and if he can bring out the man on B 3 he will win in a canter, having borne off four men already. Any 6 or 5–1 (13 shots) will take him clear. With any 4 or 3–1 he will hit on B 7 and still be favourite, though Black will have chances; for example, he may hit on W 5 when coming off the bar. On the other hand, if White rolls any combination of 2, 3 and 5 (9 shots), his back man will stay where it is, and 2–1 and 1–1 will also leave him under fire. The good shots and the bad ones about balance out, and the remainder (when he hits on B 7) are favourable. He has the necessary odds for a double but is more likely to be thinking to himself, 'If I don't come out with my next shot, and Black points on my blot, as he well may, I shall be on the bar, facing a 5-point board. Let's see what happens on my next throw'.

The answer to this line of thinking is much the same as to the argument above. In the long run it will pay White to double now and win about $\frac{2}{3}$ of the time at double stakes. If White comes out with his next throw, obviously Black won't accept a double. The principle is very common and very important: *make the opponent pay to see your bad throws.*

6 When you are too good to double

Whenever you double you give your opponent the chance to slip out for a single game. As a gammon doubles the stake automatically, it is often wrong to let your man off the hook. You are *too good* to double when:

1. You have good chances to win a gammon.
2. Your opponent would drop if you doubled.
3. There is very little chance of the game turning against you.

The third condition may look odd until you reflect that one of the prime motives for doubling is *fear*. If you might lose, then you want to force your opponent to retire.

In general, you may reckon that you have chances for a gammon when you have a 5-point prime and your opponent has two men back, or a 6-point prime against one man. A virtual 6-point prime—when the opponent will need two specific moves to escape—is also good enough. In addition, your opponent must not have a good board of his own.

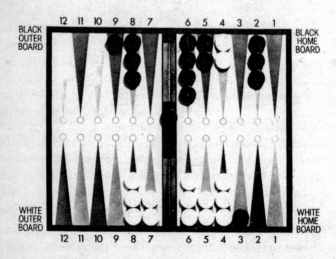

Diagram 99

White has a 5-point prime and an anchor in his opponent's board. Black has two men back, one of them on the bar, and no board of his own.

White has much too good a game to double. He will aim instead to hit the blot on W 3, to go on hitting, and to complete a prime if he can. He is not nervous of leaving a blot himself, because there is little danger of a man being contained at the back.

Suppose, however, that things were to develop poorly for White. He rolls 6–2 and makes a point at W 2. Black then rolls 3–3, his very best; he makes both 3 points and brings in the man from B 9. There are no longer any gammon chances and Black might even get back into the game (double 6 would put him well ahead). Now is the time for White to double.

7 Doubling in the end game

As the end game approaches, a count of likely throws is more signifi-cant than a count of pips, because pips do not take into account the quality of the home board and the likelihood of wasted shots. If you count by pips, seven men on the 4 point, with gaps on either side, add up to the same as three men on the 4 point and two on either side, which of course is a much better arrangement.

By the time a player begins to bear off, his count with an evenly distributed board will be about 50 to 55. If the opponent has a similar board you need the throw plus a lead of about 5 to double. If both boards are unbalanced, but the count is similar, the following are bad features: majority of men on the 6 point; any long column; majority of vacant spaces, particularly the 1 point, because if you don't fill that point you may go on missing right up to your last throw.

As there are often opportunities to double at the very end of the game, it is essential to know the chances of bearing off with various combinations. If you have formed the habit of calculating odds it is easy to assess the chances of bearing off any two men in a single throw. These are key figures:

With 5–2 (a man on 5 and a man on 2) you will be off in 19 throws, so are 19 to 17 on. This means that with 5–2 you can double an opponent who is certain to be off with his last throw. Note, however, that 4–3 (17 successful throws) and 6–1 (15 successful throws) are *not* better than 5–2; nor is 3–3 (17 throws).

(It is an interesting fact, though we don't intend to spend time on it, that it is sometimes a slight error to double even when you are odds on to win at once. This is because you will win more points if you simply throw and then take the additional chance that your opponent may miss. If you double and then miss, he will redouble and you may not be able to accept; thus you won't enjoy the combined chance of your missing and his missing as well.)

Consider next the odds about accepting when you have two men left and your opponent, who has three men on low points, doubles. You should not accept with any 9 (6–3 or 5–4); 4–4 is borderline, but you can accept with any other combination of 8 pips or less. When checking these figures, remember that the opponent will throw a double once in six, and then you won't have a chance to play.

There is one important question which arises very often: When your opponent has doubled because he has the move, to what extent may you take into account that you may save your bacon by throwing a double before he does?

Players are often advised to ignore the possibility of throwing doubles at this stage, on the grounds that the opponent is as likely to throw a double as they are. That is an over-simplification, because you are entitled to accept a double when you are just short of 3 to 1 against. Thus, if you can say to yourself, 'The chance that I will throw a double and he will not is (say) 2 to 1 against', you are entitled to accept.

The cut-off point is when there are five throws left for your opponent, as here:

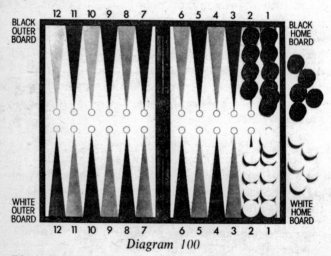

Diagram 100

Black, having the throw, will double. White may save himself if he can throw a double while his opponent does not.

128

The chance of throwing a double in two rolls is 9 to 4 against. Combining the odds for the two players, it is about $3\frac{3}{4}$ to 1 against White throwing a double in two rolls while Black does not. So far, those odds do not justify a take, but White may have further chances and these bring the odds against him below 3 to 1. Note that if White does throw a double on either of his first two turns he will be able to redouble and Black will not have a take.

8 The effect of playing backgammons

A backgammon, you may remember, occurs when at the end of the game the loser still has a man in his opponent's home board and has not borne off any man. This, when backgammons are played, is scored as a triple game. In this book we have assumed that backgammons are not being played, but you may, of course, find yourself playing in a tournament or club where they are the rule.

Except for a few freakish occasions when a player has several men on the bar and enters them very slowly, backgammons occur mostly when a player stays back on his opponent's 1 point in the hope of a shot. If backgammons are counted, it is silly to stay too long except when the opponent is down to three men on his 2 point and you have a man on the 1 point, plus a good home board. The great majority of throws will leave a blot now, and if the opponent rolls any 1 except 1–1 he will leave two blots—a position we have noted in an earlier chapter.

As a general guide, risk a backgammon when you are going to be gammoned even if you run. But if the choice is between running and losing a single game, or staying back and risking a triple game, it is advisable to run.

9 Some special odds when there is a closed board

It happens not infrequently that a player will close his board by establishing a prime from 1 to 6. It is useful to study the chances when that situation has arisen.

Suppose, first, that White has been playing a back game and has eventually scored a hit. If his opponent has only one man left, with 14 off the board, White's chances will be slim but worth playing for. If two men can be put on the bar the change is startling.

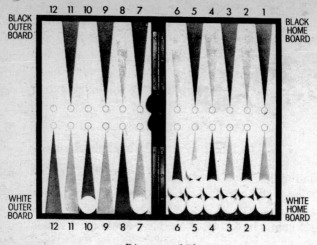

Diagram 101

White's back game has been fairly successful. He has closed his board and has managed to hit two men after Black has borne off thirteen.

What are White's chances of winning, do you think? If he plays boldly and correctly, he is about 9 to 4 on!

Having brought all his men in, White will aim first to bear off the three spare men before disturbing his prime. When he begins to leave gaps he will not follow the technique we described in Chapter 5 of bringing men down from the 6 point. Until he has about four or five men off the board he will bear off where he can, even leaving a blot on a low point. Once he has four men off, and the opponent has not entered, he can change his tactics and play more safely, because even if Black brings both men in he will need about $3\frac{1}{2}$ throws to bear each of them off the board.

This is another, more common, situation:

130

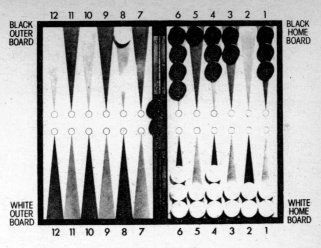

Diagram 102

Again White has a closed board and has forced two men to the bar. The question now is, what are his chances of a gammon?

The prospects of a gammon now are similar to those of a win in Diagram 101; not quite so good, because (a) White must have more regard for safety, and (b) Black may need one throw less to bring round two men and bear off another piece from any point in his board. White is still about 7 to 4 on to achieve a gammon.

The special value of these two examples is that they will enable you to assess the chances in situations which are similar. Suppose, for example, that Black, in Diagram 101, still had two men left in his home board as well as two on the bar; the odds against him would then be more than 3 to 1 and he would be wise to refuse a double.

10 'Look back in anger'

Psychology, and knowledge of the opponent's habits, play an important part in the handling of the cube. We say something about this in the next chapter. Meanwhile, we suggest a little exercise that will enable you to test your judgement. Keep a record of all the times when you have accepted a double and see how your decisions have worked out. How often have you been gammoned? How often have you lost?

How often have you won? If you have won appreciably more than once in four, you are not accepting often enough. If you have lost more than three times in four, you are accepting too many doubles.

And when you have a borderline decision at the end, note the position and study it in detail later. The value of this is that you will know how to assess similar positions another time.

CHAPTER ELEVEN

Tournaments, Chouettes and the Personal Factor

Backgammon lends itself very well to multiple events, ranging from knock-out tournaments for any number of players to informal contests for a group of three or four. The scoring and tactics in tournament play are somewhat different from those of the ordinary game.

Tournaments

The commonest form of tournament is a straight knock-out. There will usually be a sweepstake, with the proceeds going to the finalists and semi-finalists. Depending on the number of players and the time available, matches in the early rounds may be 'five points up' or 'seven points up', increasing to nine or more for the semi-final and final. The doubling cube is used, but these rules generally apply:

1. There are no automatic doubles and no beavers.
2. When one player is just one point short of victory (e.g. has scored six points in a match of 'seven up') his opponent is not allowed to double in the game immediately following. He may, if still alive, double in subsequent games. This is known as the 'Crawford rule'. It is obviously fair that a player who leads by, say, six to five should not be compelled to play 'sudden death'.

Tactics in match play

The system of scoring has an important bearing on tactics with the doubling cube. Suppose the match is 'seven up'. The early objective is to be the first to reach six (or, of course, seven), because the Crawford rule protects you from a double in the game immediately following.

133

Thus, suppose you lead by 5 to 3 and have what in an ordinary game would be a fair double. You want much better odds than usual—something like 5 to 1 in your favour. If you double, then in effect you allow the present game to decide the match. Since a doubled game would win the match for you, your opponent will immediately redouble, whatever his position. You must accept (or foolishly submit to 5 all) and then, if you lose, your opponent will take the match by 7 to 5.

The player who is behind in the early stages should be more ready to double than in an ordinary game. Suppose you trail by 5 to 3 and judge that you have a slight advantage. If you lose this game you will be 6–3 down and will probably need to win three games running. Remember that in the next game you will not be allowed to double, so you will need a gammon to improve on 4–6. You can, and will, double in the game after that, but to win the match you will still need a gammon or two more games. It follows that when you are 5–3 down, or worse, you should double whenever you have slight odds in your favour.

When your opponent stands on 6 and the Crawford rule has already operated, it is self-evident that you must double at some point in the game. It is advisable to double early. Suppose you are losing 2–6 and pull up to 3–6. If in the next game you double on your first turn, your opponent must accept or make you a present of a point. But if you delay, then have a lucky throw which puts you in a fine position, he will refuse a double and you will stand at 4–6 instead of 5–6.

Round Robin tournaments

Another form of tournament is a round robin in which, if numbers permit, all play all. One advantage is that everyone plays on equal terms throughout—you can't be knocked out or relegated to a consolation event.

Suppose you organize a party for a manageable number such as six players. You place them for the first round as follows:

A   F   E   **A** is the stationary player. The others move as a chain in a clockwise direction, so that **A** plays C on the second round, D on the third, and so on.

B   C   D

With five rounds to play, you might make each round consist of five games. Allowing for the fact that you will have to wait for the slowest table, you may estimate about fifty minutes for a round. On that basis the tournament will last a little over four hours.

Scoring is by points and the winner is the player who scores the highest number of points. There are no automatic doubles but gammons count in the usual way. In some tournaments of this kind no doubling is allowed, on the grounds that one game amounting to 16 points or more would have a disproportionate effect on the result. However, the game seems very flat when the cube is not in use, and a reasonable compromise is to allow two doubles in one game but not more.

When there are too many players for all to meet all, the system is to set out two long rows, calling the players on one side North, on the other, South. The North players remain stationary and the South players move along as a chain, playing three games against each opponent for a number of rounds to be determined in advance.

Duplicate tournaments

In this type of event the tables are set up as for a round robin and the dice to be played by North and South are called out from the platform. Scoring and movement are the same as for a round robin. It is necessary to set a time limit, or a limit of moves, for each game, and unfinished games may require adjudication.

This may be an amusing, even an instructive, exercise, but it does not eliminate the factor of luck in the way that duplicate bridge eliminates the luck of the deal. Once the moves at different tables have begun to diverge, as assuredly they will, a throw that is excellent for North at one table may be very bad for him at another.

Chouettes

A chouette is a form of contest in which three, four, or even more players may take part although there is only one table in play. The dictionary meaning of this French word is 'screech-owl', but it is also used as an endearment (make what you like of that!). Its relation to the present form of encounter is obscure.

Suppose there are four players in the game. They each throw one die, rolling again to break any ties. The player with the highest number goes 'into the box' and, until defeated, plays against the other three. The player who threw the second highest die plays the first game and is described as the 'captain'. During the game the captain is the final arbiter (except in the matter of doubles, as explained below), but he may consult with his partners whenever he is doubtful about the best play. Within limits, the partners may proffer advice when they disagree with the play that the captain proposes to make. Once the dice have been picked up, however, the move stands unless it was an illegal move and the opponent chooses to point this out before making his next throw.

The scoring and movement of players

If the man in the box wins a first game of, say, 4 points, he goes down on the score-sheet as plus 12 and each of his opponents stands at minus 4. Having won the game, this player stays in the box and the next man on the list takes over as player and captain.

Suppose that the second game is won by the 'partners'. The man who played the game goes into the box and the fourth man on the original list plays opposite him as captain. The player who has left the box goes to the bottom of the list, and so the series continues. The player in the box always has three opponents (in a four-sided game), so wins or loses three times the value of the game. Gammons count in the usual way.

Doubles

When the man in the box doubles (or redoubles), the captain will consult with his partners, who will say whether they wish to accept or refuse. Any player may drop out, losing the number of points shown on the cube before the double. If the man in the box is agreeable, another player in the team may take over the game of the player who has resigned, taking the points he owes and settling for him at the finish of the game. Players who have dropped out cease to be partners and may not be consulted. If the captain drops out, another player takes over and goes into the box if he wins.

There is no fixed procedure for doubles made by the partners. In some games the captain will not double unless all his partners agree. In others, any player who does not wish to participate in the double may be bought out. Suppose the cube stands at 4 and the captain wishes to make it 8, but one of the players won't go along with him. The captain (or another partner) may say, 'I'll take over your game and pay you out (say) 2 points'. The deal may be agreed, but the man in the box may pre-empt the offer, saying 'I'll give you 2 points and you are out of the game'. It comes to this, that any game may be settled at any time for any price, but the box may pre-empt any deal at the price offered.

Stakes in a chouette

One writer describes a chouette as 'a more social form of backgammon'. That is one side of the picture. Any game may of course be played in a friendly and social spirit, but chouettes have a special appeal for gamblers because of the chance of a big winning run when in the box. In the London clubs the top players will usually be seen playing a chouette.

The same writer remarks that chouette is 'particularly suited to beginners because poorer players have a better chance of winning'. Don't be too sure of that! When playing as captain, with others to advise him, the beginner is playing for the standard stake, but when he goes into the box he is on his own and playing for two or three times the usual amount. Scores, obviously, run much higher than in a straight game between two players. It is quite possible to lose 100 units in a long session; possible, also, to win 200. If one player wishes to play at a lower stake than the others, he may, by agreement, play for half the normal stake when in the box.

The personal factor

Skill, chance and personality all play a big part in backgammon. It would have been distracting, in our account of the game, to say, 'Play this move against one opponent, this against another', but such distinctions do of course exist.

We are not thinking so much of the opponent's *style* of play. The best move is the best move whether the other man is aggressive or cautious, traditional or modern. There are two respects in which personality is important: your opponent's general ability, relative to your own; and his handling of the cube.

Playing against stronger or weaker opponents

Suppose you are playing 'seven up' against an opponent whom you know to be a better and more experienced player. You should start from the assumption that you are unlikely to win by normal, conservative play. If you are lucky enough to win the opening throw, make one of the aggressive openings. With 6–5 or 6–4, for example, don't play Moscow to Vladivostock (B 1 to B 12) or Moscow to Nijninovgorod

(B1 to B11), but play to your bar point and to W8 or W9, as the case may be. If you escape a hit you have a good chance to establish an early advantage. From then on, play a solid game, hoping for at least equal luck with the dice.

Be, if anything, more bold with the doubling cube than you would be against an opponent of equal strength. Remember that things have got to go your way for you to win. If you find yourself with the better game early on, don't be afraid to double; and if your opponent doubles you in a borderline situation, don't think, 'I am likely to lose this game, so I'll go quietly'. Think instead, 'Perhaps things will turn my way and I'll be able to redouble before the game ends'.

Against a weaker opponent, avoid the speculative openings and consider the general situation after a dozen moves. If your opponent has made a good start, make the game more difficult by playing 'control moves', as explained in Chapter 7; he won't know how to deal with them. Be conservative with the cube. To beat you, he has got to win seven points, and this he will find difficult. You don't want to make close doubles and see one throw turn the game, as can easily happen. So, make him go the full distance.

Tactics with the doubling cube

As we remarked in the last chapter, the way the cube is handled marks the difference between players of roughly equal ability; and in this area psychology plays an important part.

Almost all players have little quirks that cause their judgement to vary from centre. Some are over-cautious in offering and accepting doubles; their theory is that so long as they avoid losing the big games they will come out on top. Others accept too often and probably know it. Some players, when a lot down in a session, will play a very nervous game; others will gamble wildly, beavering and redoubling, in an attempt to get their losses back.

Your task is to identify—not difficult—and then exploit these variations from the norm. If your opponent is always ready to lie down to a double, double him constantly until he begins to doubt his judgement. If he is the (more common) type who accepts too often, delay your double until you have good odds in your favour.

As for your own game, the ideal is to have no quirks, to keep a level head and judge every situation on its merits whether you are a heavy loser or a big winner. If you can play to the odds, they won't let you down.

At the same time, it is wise to recognize that scarcely one player in a hundred can play his best game when losing heavily and you are probably not that player. Best is to stop and wait for another day; if that's difficult, play a conservative but not a nervous game. On the other hand, if you are in a big winning run, the odds are that you are playing better than your opponent.

You will note that we say 'playing better', not 'playing in form', a phrase that suggests you are in luck and will continue to be. You may know it's your lucky day; but do the dice know?

Handicaps

When one player is admittedly stronger than the other, it is easy to arrange a fair handicap. One method is to allow the weaker player a strong opening move such as 3–1 or 6–1. When the difference is more marked, the stronger player may concede odds over a short series of games. For example, he may lay 6 to 4 over three games. If after three games he is 3 points up he wins three times the stake, but if he is three down he loses four-and-a-half times the stake and a new series begins with the same conditions.

Playing for money

It is not our business to tell anyone how to look after his money, but we can make a few objective comments about backgammon.

To begin with, it has a high skill factor. Despite the number of games that seem to hang on a single throw, despite the games that depend on who has the luck to throw a double when bearing off, despite the games that are decided by a single pip—despite all that, backgammon is primarily a game of skill, not of chance. A poorish bridge or poker player will win perhaps three or four sessions out of ten, which is bad enough; but a backgammon player who is outclassed will be lucky to win more than once in ten sessions of three or four hours' play.

For this reason, and because of its appearance of manifold chances, backgammon is a great game for hustlers, amateur or professional. One feature of the hustler's game is that he will always be ready to lie down to a double when his opponent has made a good start. The last thing he wants is a long struggle which he may even lose. The session won't last for ever and time is important. 'Besides', one of them was heard to remark, 'with a little encouragement my man may want to increase the stakes'.

Index